How Lovely Are Thy Dwellings

Brynmor Pierce Jones
MA BD DipEd

How Lovely are Thy Dwellings
by
Brynmor Pierce Jones

ISBN 0 9536657 0 4

Second Edition

Published by:

Wellspring
39, Pillmawr Circle
Malpas
Newport
NP20 6WP

Formerly a school teacher and a college lecturer in Religious Studies, Rev. Brynmor Jones, now retired, has pastored the Rogerstone Mission Hall, Trosnant, Glascoed and Raglan Baptist Churches. He was led to the Lord by humble servants of the King and nurtured spiritually in churches encouraging consecration. Educated in the Rhondda Valley he obtained Honours degrees in English and History and later obtained a third degree, plus an MA.

He was constrained by the Lord to chronicle church history around the time of the Welsh Revival. This book is the sixth chronicle. His prayer is that these stories will give spiritual uplift as well as a personal challenge.

Shortly after completing this book, the author went to be with his Lord and Saviour in Glory. We thank the Lord for the strength given to complete the book that He had so clearly given to Brynmor to write.

Dedication

To my faithful and loving wife

With thanks

I would like to express heartfelt thanks to my son Colin, who has spent long hours publishing and printing this book and to my wife for her painstaking typing and editing.

With appreciation for the support of the committee of the Keswick in Wales Convention through prayer; contribution to content; publicity and proof reading.

To those people through whom the book will be distributed.

Disclaimer

Whilst considerable effort has been expended to ensure that the factual contents of this book are accurate, the limitations of the 'personal testimony' research methodology are also recognised. We apologise for any inaccuracies that may exist and would welcome corrections in order that future editions can be amended.

Contents

Table of Photographs

1 *A Brief History of Separations*

The world-wide fast-growing flock which we call the 'Manifold Kingdom of Christ,' has always contained within itself little clusters of sheep which have quite distinctive marks. Sometimes an under-shepherd comes along and quietly draws away one such cluster. Sometimes we see an impatient ram detach several ewes and take his followers towards other green pastures. One such group will always make for a more open field, yet another one will always make for a little sheltered corrie, or a high-walled enclosure. The first group we can interpret symbolically as movements and the second group as sects.

These divisive processes were not unknown in the first centuries in the Christian era and it caused confusion and failure as numerous sects sprang up. No doubt, there were splinter groups in the Middle Ages also; people like the Albigensians and the hated followers of John Hus.

The great division occurred in protestant circles where freethinking Zwingli and the radical Mennonites and Anabaptists left the Calvinists, who tried to stop them from wandering from the fold. One hundred years later we also find Quakers and Fifth Monarchists in England, Pietists and Moravians in Germany. In the 19th century, Britain had Primitive Methodists, Bible Christians and the Salvation Army, who all came out of Methodism in order to be free to pursue their different visions. In Scotland also there were secessions, such as the 'Wee Frees.' America could furnish more colourful movements such as the Dukhubors and the Shakers.

The new feature of the late nineteenth century breakaways was that each group would passionately endorse a specific doctrine, which they claimed by special revelation. One group might advocate a totally democratic fellowship of believers as all priests unto God. One group might proclaim the 'Imminent Return of Christ' and the 'End of the World.' One group might major on 'Holiness' and another on the 'Infallibility of the Scriptures.' One or two groups went badly astray, for example Irvingites and Russellites. Other groups really came into their own when both New Theology and the German-born 'Higher Criticism of the Sacred Text' made deep wounds in the Creed and the Bible of the mainline Christian Church. As we saw in the revised edition of 'Kings Champions' the liberals were generally anti-revivalist and devised various ways to stifle it as soon as possible. This was bound to breed in its turn some strong reactive movements expressing the more vigorous and dogmatic forms of conservatism in thought and practice.

The struggle had begun already in 1906-1908 when converted church officers at Llanon were dismissed. A Gorseinon group was denounced because they spoke against the New Theology adopted by their minister, and a youth prayer Fellowship was shut out of a Loughor chapel because their pre-service prayer times took too long and made them late. Another group at Felinfoel was expunged from the church roll after they had requested second baptism by water because they felt that their teenage one had been insincere. The battle hotted up when some of these newly ejected groups claimed that by their obedience they had received the fullness of the Spirit in order to have such powers to witness that "the gates of hell will not prevail against us."

In the first and second decades of this century, there was a further tremendous disturbance of the main flock by a vibrant force called the 'Tongues Movement' or the 'Signs Movement.' The leaders and prophets claimed to be ushering in the 'Third Age,' the 'Pentecost Age.' This was the 'Dispensation of the Holy Spirit.' At once, some called them wolves and serpents, some called them tares and some called them deluded and deceptive. Yet others were convinced they were purifiers and light-bringers, bringing into prominence the much needed doctrines of 'New Birth' and 'Baptism in the Spirit.' Unlike other movements they expected misunderstanding and opposition from the first.

In South Wales the vast majority of ordinary Christians had always stayed within the established denominations. The sects named earlier on had made very little headway beyond the easternmost towns. Even the 'Forward Movement,' led by Seth Joshua, failed to set up many bases in the Welsh valleys, whilst the Brethren stuck to the cities of the coast.

About 1912, there was an official survey of the religions in Wales. Alongside the traditional Churches there were strange “folds” called Gospel Halls, Mission Halls and Cottage Fellowships. How had these Gospel Halls come into being? What was their purpose? The common factor was that each place was owned and used by one of the many groups of ‘born again’ people who wanted more freedom, spirituality and certainty.

From 1905 onwards, each of these halls had its mixture of new born lambs, who had never been inside any other fold, with much older sheep who had found a new freedom and joy after they yielded to the Holy Spirit. Amongst them, also, were former church leaders who had served and taught their churches well, but had suddenly been rejected. In some districts, the ‘dyed in the wool’ members had turned around and harassed those who had been most keen about new forms of worship and witness. Dr. Morris of Treorchy had severe things to say about religious hierarchies who had first criticised the Revival and then suggested ways to control the dangerous new tendencies. Having attended high level conferences in the autumn of 1906, he gave this verdict on the Church leaders.

> "These men had not experienced the kiss of the tender breeze from Calvary, and had not felt the strength of the mighty wind of Pentecost. Some are entire strangers to the Spirit and we marvel to hear them talk.”

The strength and energy of the counter-Revival currents will be understood far better from a new chapter in the revised ‘King's Champions.’ They drew in the COPEC Conferences, the Summer Schools for Sunday school teachers, the first manuals for newly arrived ministers. Each of the central doctrines was re-examined and challenged in the name of freedom of study and communication. These new men were soon filling the chief posts in the Colleges, in the Churches and in the Religious Publishing Houses. They had influence in appointing many a minister who had received a good education, but had been insulated from the Welsh Revival during their student years. Revival converts felt they were resented and disowned because of over passionate worship or overzealous evangelism or some other cause. The worst of all was that so many ordinary members had preferred to get back to what they called 'normality.' The Rev. R. B. Jones forewarned converts that they would be treated as a slighted but dangerous minority.

> "As He was, so must you be ready to be called 'transgressors,' or be held up to contempt in the Press, or among acquaintances. Why should you resent this? Do you really want to have the good opinion of the world. I thought you had given up loving the applause of the world. So! Why resent being misrepresented?"

Some groups got into trouble simply by letting compassion rule their lives. They went out into the highways and byways and sought to rescue children and hitherto unreached adults. It wasn't long before their home churches passed resolutions demanding that they stopped these activities and concentrated on their home churches - or else withdrew membership.

About 50% of the new missions began with expulsions, but another 25% withdrew voluntarily in search of a more welcoming atmosphere. The remaining 25% were set up a little later to accomplish specific tasks or to defend and re-assert particular biblical truths. In this extensive survey of the Halls we shall have to be careful to distinguish between the different kinds of Mission and note any changes in purpose and scope. At this preliminary stage we can state that many pre-Revival and post-Revival Mission Halls had a strong evangelistic drive.

But there were others whose dominant aim was to guard and to guarantee that the 'conservative' tradition stayed inviolate. They announced that they would expect all members to subscribe to a strictly defined 'Confession of Faith' and never to modify it. Conversely there was a smaller number who believed passionately that they should seek first to be filled with the Spirit whatever the cost. All of these types can be found side by side in the industrial belt that stretches from Pontypool to Carmarthen.

The process of separation and division that began in 1910 became acute after the 1914-1918 war and can be said to have continued until recent times. The F.I.E.C. Missions, the Irish Missions and Church planters from the USA, have perhaps caused such discontinuity that it is well nigh impossible to see the original shape and purpose of the Halls which they took over. This picture was given by Mr. A. S. Rogers about ten years later.

"If some Churches had dealt fairly with the Revival and had welcomed and succoured those who were awakened and blessed through it, some of these Gospel halls would not be in existence today. Hard, cold churches, resisting the Holy Spirit, are accountable for the existence of so many of these places found today in Carmarthenshire and Glamorgan. Not all these Halls have stayed faithful to the Gospel in its simplicity. We are sorry to say that some have turned from the great central road of the Gospel of Grace. Despite this, there are some to be found which are worthy of their title - Gospel Halls. Recently we had the privilege of spending two days among the people of one of these Halls and of preaching the Word to them."

Rogers clearly distrusted the new crop of Pentecostalist Halls that appeared in the twenties - led by Dan Williams, Stephen Jeffreys and Hutchinson. The older leaders had lost their vision and diverted into 'Fundamentalism' and 'Second Adventism.' R.B. Jones' idea of creating 'Citadel Churches' to guard the truth was not generally accepted. The Lord took away the anointing and the power so that each part of revived religion weakened once more. Both the breakaways and the opposition stemmed from this rejection of Revival blessing against which both R. B. Jones and Evan Roberts protested. R. B. Jones wrote,

"Is there not something terribly amiss when those born of the Holy Spirit, who receive Life from the same Lord Jesus and who pray to the same Heavenly Father, are unable to sit down together to worship in one place? Whence these endless divisions? Have they not come about because we have more zeal than love, and because we put more stress on circumstantials than on essentials; on the gifts of God, rather than the Giver; on signs rather than faith?

"Zeal is nothing but a terrible renderer when there isn't enough love to balance it. Let us all earnestly seek to be baptized in perfect love for one another - that love which can embrace a brother even if he cannot agree on every point of faith."

Evan Roberts was so disturbed by this divisive tendency that he wrote a kind of pattern prayer in 1912, which had to be reprinted on request in 1924. This pattern prayer may well have been intended as a model for the numerous members of the Prayer Bond.

> "Let the peaceable wisdom from on high dominate my actions. Let not my thoughts disturb the peace of Thy Church in causing schisms, quarrels and divisions, unbearable to Thee and detrimental to the Living Church. Let all the church walk in sweet fellowship with Christ and with one another."

Figure 1: Llanpumpsaint Caretakers Revival Prayer Meeting

2 *The Birth of Pentecostalism in Wales*

The two mission churches and their offshoots were rightly regarded as the prototypes of revival converts' Mission Halls. Their story shows all the strengths and weaknesses of the new movements. Penygroes was then a semi-rural area where the skylarks were as numerous and noisy as the hooters. Revival blew into this village through the 1906 Prayer Meetings and the united revival services, then held in the Independent Chapel. Many a visiting brother dropped in to tell them about the great blessing at the nearby town of Ammanford.

The members all decided to hold united Prayer meetings where men and women poured out their heartfelt longings. A woman, who always wore a red cap, led these passionate prayers. The news that a woman had been praying aloud was noised abroad so that more and more people were coming. By the third week, a very sober deacon was seen clapping before the Lord and they all went on fire. A Mr. Rees Evans remembered dozens of such services with crying, weeping and simultaneous praying. The Glory of God filled the place. The fruit of this was that, on one Sunday alone, close on 120 sought the right hand of fellowship.

In time the Pentecostalist groups began to feel they had to separate to achieve their desires. They had all agreed at one time to one mission and message, but now they wanted their own worship patterns and testimony. The good-natured debate carried on for three years until misunderstandings and criticisms arose. Certain cold souls took over the regular services and the 'Children of the Revival' were refused permission to conduct services in their own style. Meanwhile a decision was being made by the majority group to appoint twelve trustees to build a new Hall, instead of a borrowed vestry. This was intended to be undenominational and would undertake many missions. This brave group met on the 3rd Sunday in August, 1907 and decided to draw up a confession of faith, which included the Second birth, full assurance of Salvation, Sanctification and the Second Coming/Rapture. It excludes speaking in tongues as a doctrine. (See Appendix A.)

The late Mr. Meurig Thomas and his family fortunately preserved the rules and regulations of this prototype Mission Hall. The 1907 Welsh document, together with the 1953 English version (produced for a new body of trustees), provide our best guide to the vision and methods of the converts. Indeed it is our only guide because of certain restrictions affecting early Mission Halls. Many readers may wonder why we cannot give any figures for membership or for giving and why we cannot find a written Constitution. We have had to respect the genuine belief of the Founders of these Halls that it was quite unscriptural to make registers of attendees or to make written records of gifts. Most had no Annual Reports either. So the occasional National Surveys of Wales ignored them.

Rules and regulations for management of a non-sectarian Hall, framed under the provision of the Trust (14th October, 1909), permitting the erection of a Mission Hall to be used for non-sectarian purposes in accordance with principles, framed by the trustees or by a committee, appointed by them. They stated that,

> *The people who assemble at the Evangelistic Church are to be responsible for all expenses of upkeep and maintenance of the Mission Hall and outbuildings in decent condition. They are also to be responsible for all expenses incurred as necessary in all matters arising from time to time, in accordance with the Rules and Regulations from time to time, framed by the Trustees under the powers of the said Trust Deed.*
>
> *Further to these rules, in order that the Trustees may attend to and pay for certain items of expense and cost in relation to the structure of the said Mission Hall and outbuildings, the Trustees will impose a weekly rent. This will be paid on the usual quarter days of each year, commencing as from the 1st. January.*
>
> *Extra regulations shall be devised, stating times of meetings, notice of meetings, quorums, Chairman's term of office. Finally - the decision of the majority of the trustees present must be binding and shall be signed as conclusive evidence of all that went on in the meeting.*

A large group broke away only a year later and formed a new venture called the Tabernacle or Pabell, after meeting for several months in an old hut. Groups, from a wider district, went to special Conferences at Sunderland seeking the Baptism of the Holy Ghost with signs, e.g. speaking in tongues. They were promised new, high experiences as they entered a new dispensation. At first, the two groups shared together, but then the 'refusers' of these extra blessings were called 'smoking flax' and 'cold irons.' One leader, Rees Evans, made more militant noises, but the Mission Hall trustees denied any such claims and described the new system as from Hell and not from God and so, from here on, the Penygroes community was hopelessly divided. Members of the progressive group were eventually excommunicated for transgressing the rules. Because many of them had contributed generously to the building costs of the first Hall, it was argued and eventually agreed that they should receive some compensation when they went their own way. In 1913, the two friends, R. B. Jones and W. S. Jones were asked to arbitrate and they negotiated a division of the fund which was wise and amicable. The Rev. W. S. Jones inserted a typical spiritual message.

"Let everything be done in order, in meekness of spirit and in the love of the LORD."

No blame should be laid on Daniel Powell Williams who remained as a recognised pastor of a Congregational Church until sorely troubled by apostles from America, who were openly proclaiming "The Baptism and Fullness of the Spirit" as the key to service and power. He began, also, to receive prophetic messages, such as,

"I have brought you here, for My purposes concerning thee are great. My hand have I laid upon thee for a work.

"In that day thou shalt be called David in My sight and not Daniel, because of the battles thou shalt go through."

"Go to your brother's house and cause W. Jones Williams to be a fellow- traveler and co-worker."

What was ultimately planned was a visit to South Wales fellowships from Penygroes via Pontardulais, Swansea, Neath and Pontypridd. He wanted to offer fellowship, guidance and support to little groups but the Lord said, "Not yet!"

A few years later, - about 1916-1919 and about 1920-1922, he went a' journeying. Meanwhile he had been given a special task at Penygroes.

> "God has declared here tonight that there will be a temporal blessing on Penygroes because there is a revolving-engine room of the Eternal purpose going on here. When power came to Penygroes we could not understand it; we could not control it. We could not rule. So the tide went back for a little. But now the called of the Lord are on this mount. There was a visitation with speaking in tongues and healings to a small company who all had a simple trust in God. I was the smallest of that tribe. Now in this time we see the rings from God's screw spread wide and we shall touch the whole globe."

It is simply a matter of history that the Apostolic 'Pabell' and College became the centre from which 'The Apostolic Churches of Wales and the World' have spread out. Certain ceremonies always take place there, - such as the laying-on of hands for new pastors and a little known ceremony involving a beautiful horn-shaped vase for anointing. It seems to be a symbol of God's outpoured Power, which kept alive their witness.

While D. P. Williams was on his 1916-1919 trek through South Wales, there was a further split in 1916. Those who were impressed by W.B. Hutchinson of Bournemouth's claims to be the first apostle to Wales, decided they must accept his system. So they had adopted the model, set out in Ephesians ch.4 v.8-15 and had already designated Omri Jones - pastor, John Evans - overseer, and Caleb Morgan. They paid excessive respect to their men and women prophets, such as Mrs. Kenny, who warned them that they would endure persecution. This was not true at Penygroes where the local school board gave them the use of the schoolrooms. Like everyone else, they bought and erected a wooden hall. They had a symbolic gift on the table - a very old Bible presented by a founder and elder, William Thomas, who had his photograph inscribed on a page. Possibly they also possessed a Horn of Blessing which was used on rare occasions.

All three groups, evangelistic, apostolic and Hutchinsonian, retained their power as witnesses and we shall meet with them again at Pontardulais, Crosshands and Pantyffynnon. However one must admit that there was a loss of vision and energy and a tendency to become more dogmatic and separatist at the same time as new denominational ministers in the traditional Chapels became more outspoken in advocating the New Theology.

Figure 2: Public Revival Worship

3

Evidence from Pembrokeshire is very slim but one witness has made a brief reference to some kind of Mission at Hook, whilst another spends a few words on a Mission at Kilgetty common where gypsy encampments could be reached. Major Russell, in his book, 'The One-by-one Band,' says that a Mr. Thomas had set up a centre in order to attract young people from the outlying hamlets.

Carmarthen

A small number of Independent Missions flourished for a while in this ancient borough. The beginnings of a mission here have now come to light in a strange way. The ageing Pastor Bapstone of Raglan Baptist Church, felt led to write out his personal testimony. Somehow, this was inserted in the Church records before these were deposited in the Baptist safe.

As a young man Mr. Bapstone clearly had special visionary experiences of the Lord, so much so, that his sister noticed that his hair and clothes were soaked with perspiration as he cried out "I have seen the Lord." He was heard to exult and praise more than once. Filled with this Spirit, he moved down to Carmarthen and joined Lamas Street Chapel. He says that he used every opportunity to beg, borrow, buy, study and apply the religious classics along with his Bible. By 1875, he was ready for active service and now found a Mission house conducted by the hard-pressed John Mortimer. He first tested Bapstone as a street preacher in the open air at the Crossways in Water Street. Those, powerfully affected by the messages, were visited in their own homes.

After John Mortimer's health broke, the younger man took over and held the fort until some local Church leaders found a replacement, who could preach in Welsh as well as English. He does not name his successor, but we hear of a Mr. John as Mission leader just before the Welsh Revival. About 1902, Major Russell, of the One-by-one Band, took a Mission in Carmarthen and was assisted by an R. Gregory, who had come to the Lord in that Mission Hall. A year later there was a visit by a Bible teacher, called Reader Harris, who held a 'Holiness Convention.'

After the Revival blessings of 1905, converts continued to use the old mission but they did not remain together. In the 1920's some would be attending the Blue Street Mission who would be teaching full assurance and the Second Coming. The other group formed Mill Street Free Mission, in the street called Heol Dam. They made the usual choice between close disciplined instruction and the free expression and sharing of experiences. All converts and members supported the open-air witness in the cattle market and believed that the Holy Spirit would honour this. Both these groups found excellent new accommodation in due course.

Welsh converts who wished to stay in ordinary chapel membership soon found that their special prayer meetings were cancelled and their youth teams of witness were never sent anywhere, not even the girls who could sing and testify. "They were all silenced," said 98 year old David Jones of Blaenporth near Newquay. They needed somewhere to express their liberty from traditional forms of worship.

New Halls

They began to build Mission Halls on the pleasant hills between Carmarthen and Cardigan. One of these was set up at Llangeler and another at Hermon. The most striking of these was Bryn Moriah on the hills far above Cynwyl Elfed. It came into being as the only solution to a cleavage between the converts and the existing chapel members. The converts wished to carry on the same kind of worship as in 1905 - shouting, weeping, exulting, confessing private sins publicly. The existing chapel members tried to subdue them and then made it clear that they were not wanted. They worked sacrificially until they could open a debt-free Hall. So bitter were the feelings that nearby farmers debarred the wagons and carriages of visitors on the Dedication day and refused to feed and water their horses. Those chapels are in difficulties but the Bryn Moriah Hall still functions actively.

Many chapel leaders, who had shut their eyes and ears to the Revival blessing, now resumed their 'normal' programme. They took steps to suppress and cut out all those who continued to worship exuberantly and who were pressing for more spirituality. The silenced ones would usually create a Mission of their own but not always. A few miles from Cynwyl Elved was the village of Llanpumpsaint where the Revival converts had met quietly in the School House, then managed by a Mrs. Morris. For two generations it fulfilled God's purposes for it and God honoured them by granting them another localised revival. The result was another group of converted farmers. A friend, who was teaching in Cardigan and who is a child of the Cwmtwrch Mission, had fellowship with that group and recalled how warmly he had been welcomed in 1965. Their mission consisted of personal witness and praying for Revival, not another Hall.

If you travel eastwards via Llanybyther you come to the little village of Talley and the little chapel called Halfway which has upheld an evangelical witness ever since they wrote an appeal in the Llanelli Mercury, asking that some of the Revival team should come to the village. The last time we passed that way we noticed that it had been refurbished and brightened up and that it declared its evangelical stance quite boldly. It decided to affiliate with the Apostolic Church of Wales.

There was also an independent cause at Pontyates and some kind of evangelistic outreach - a kind of Gospel Tent Mission, reaching the villages in the Gwendraeth Valleys. Women converts took tracts around each village and sometimes gave their testimonies. Visiting evangelists such as William Phillips helped the men. It gradually became pentecostalised.

There is no sign of penetration into the Towy valley except at Llandeilo where a Mr. Thomas, petrol merchant, prepared the ground. There were small causes at Llanarthney and Dryslwyn. There is an old account of near-riot conditions, especially near Llandybie. Someone spread a rumour that a newly-arrived group of Pentecostals were Belgian farmers, who had come to take over a tract of arable land, just as 'foreigners' from 'Herefordshire' had left their failed orchards and had come to Tonmawr near Neath.

Kidwelly

While some evangelists travelled from the upland Mission Halls down the Gwendraeth Valley, via Pontyates, other evangelistic teams were working northwards from Kidwelly. The Kidwelly Mission began life as services in the open field on Coleman's farm, sometimes followed by a tea. An 'Echoes of Grace' reporter wrote,

> "They all sat on the green grass while the 'Bread of Life' was broken. The Joy of the Lord was their strength. On one occasion five of them gave their names for baptism. While they were praising there were two women upon whom the Holy Ghost fell. They were baptised in the Spirit and magnified God."

There was no need of a rented room or Hall until the Colemans had given up their farm and moved back to Swansea.

Cross Hands

At the northern edge of that valley, stood Cross Hands village where the east-west and the north-south roads first linked. The believers had quite a struggle setting up there. They had to accept the help of Bryn Seion, Ammanford Gospel Hall and the oldest Evangelical Hall at Penygroes. Some of the full Pentecostals came witnessing and weeping at their meetings. There was a double witness once more before they agreed to divide. The Pentecostals would have gone with Jacob Skym from Brynseion to set up their work. The other Mission was closely associated with Edward Wilkins, an ex-missionary who came out from Bryn Seion and began a new work, aided by William Herbert of Ammanford. Mr. Wilkins had served the Lord abroad for a short while but helped to establish Cross Hands Gospel Hall in 1907. Using the 'Star Pub' as his base he preached from street to street as far as Pontyberem. This important founder was once described as 'a Christian gentleman in the garb of a common worker, with the marks of Divine grace seen clearly in his life.'

Maesybont

We are indebted to a Christian friend for his personal memories of this little Mission Hall, Hebron, to the north of Crosshands. His grandfather and his great-uncle were expelled from the C.M. Chapel as disturbers. They devised the deeds and chose the trustees for the New Mission. They were determined that their Fellowship should be characterised by a loving concern for each other, by the holy kiss between sisters and by a bold testimony and fervent public praise. As late as the 1950's, they ran open-air services down as far as Llanddarog. Mr. Perkins also preached in the market in Llandeilo at the end of market day. One man went to the farms around Llanarthney. Finally there were visiting evangelists like Dan Jones, who preached in marquees during the summer months. Until the 'Fires' went out they were very fruitful.

Figure 3: Hebron Hall at Maes-y-bont near Cross Hands

"The halls at Maesybont, Tycroes, Pantyffynnon and Penygroes were very similar, being plain on the outside but stylized inside with a well raised rostrum within each. Verses were the main adornment on the wall behind the pulpit. The tables below the pulpit were used for the Breaking of Bread, but they could be used for general purposes. If there was a central aisle with two rows of pews, it was often the case that the brothers would sit on one side and the sisters on the other. The pews in Maesybont, like those in Penygroes would double up as tables. These were needed for the many meals that they enjoyed together, especially on the Lord's Day, when many would stay in the Hall all day rather than walk home and return. They were needed in monthly

United Bible Studies, in annual Preaching Services and other events. Now there are organs and pianos in all Halls whereas his father had only a tuning fork in the early days. They used William Herbert's bilingual hymnbook 'Hymnau o Fawl' (Hymns of Praise). The first edition contained only hymns relating to the Lord's Sufferings, Death, Resurrection and Coming in Glory.

Order of Services in Maesybont

1. Lord's Day morning. i.e. The Lord's Supper with most of the brothers taking part. All hymns and Scripture readings were to be Spirit-led.

2. Lord's Day afternoon. First the Sunday School for the children, and then the Bible Class.

3. Lord's Day tea-time. A short service broadcast on loudspeakers outside the Hall, audible seven miles away.

4. Lord's Day evening. Gospel Meeting to a packed out Hall. This would include a Testimony meeting and then several brothers would preach.

5. Prayer Meetings. Tuesday for the men, Wednesday for the women and Thursday for everybody. Finally, Saturday was for Tract Distribution, banner carrying and an open-air Meeting. The Keynote was fervour and commitment."

6. One veteran remembered that, if the service was in a summertime marquee, they could use other ex-army equipment, including a bugle.

One of the helpers, Dafydd Daniel, a convert from the Revival put it neatly, in a commemorative service, "I still feel the power of the Resurrection in my soul as I was transported from death into life."

Pantyffynnon

The original building was quite small, but it was replaced by a more substantial one, which was the responsibility of a group similar to the Brethren. Throughout the years, it has kept up a quiet witness, yet recently there have been signs of new life and activity. It is on the corner between the main Llandeilo road and two lanes.

Gorslas and Gorsgoch

A borrowed hut was used in the winter months for those unable to get to Penygroes in the terrible weather on those hills. A photograph, taken when the larger hut replaced the first one, shows that it resembled a barrack room. Gradually, other people came to join them, including some that clearly preferred an Apostolic emphasis.

Figure 4: Ex Army Hut used by Gorsgoch and Gorslas

Cwmgwili

The founder's son is still alive and he recalls that it was a very small building, holding 120 chairs, but no pews or pulpit or even a communion table. The children and the League met in a small Sunday Schoolroom and there was also a well-attended Bible Class. Not much attention was paid there to Singing Schools but they loved to use 'Llyfrau'r Diwygiad' i.e. Revival booklets containing Revival Songs. On principle they held no membership roll and had no annual meetings or business meetings. Women could take part in prayer and testimony, but there were a few other restrictions from the beginning. The Lords Gift Box at the back of the Hall covered all the Hall's expenses and ministry. Members were required to hold a few essential doctrines but they never stressed believers' baptism. They never seemed to link with formal organisations though many went annually to the Llandrindod Convention.

This congregation is aged now and very quiet and sedate. Their Mission Hall produced some very special fruit such as Lizzie Mary Rees and Dewi Griffiths, missionaries.

Tycroes Gospel Hall

It seems strange that this district acquired Gospel Halls at a time when the distinguished preacher, Robert Ellis, was faithfully presenting Revival truths and visions. But he was in the Welsh chapel and now there was a flood of English speaking families who needed a place of worship and instruction. One of the Mission centres is associated with the name of Jacob Skym, ex-Bryn Seion, who lived in Upper Tumble. Much more is known about the first Hall near Tycroes because of the magazine 'Riches of Grace.' Another magazine, called 'Echoes of Grace,' describes each step of their way. Their first article said:

> "The Word of the Lord is not bound. He has graciously blessed us with a Hall, which will hold one hundred and fifty. The servants of Satan have sought to destroy the testimony in various ways, but no man shall hinder. This hall stands as an eloquent testimony to the Lord's visitation."

Acts of witness were taking place in the main street in the days of Eddie Wilkins and Lewis Rees. However, the main growth period was in 1923-1924, when the well-known Evangelists, Clarke and Bell, held a long mission in Ammanford and Penygroes. For the first time their Bible teachers gave up their traditional way of expounding the scriptures to take a simpler approach in order to encourage and nurture the newcomers.

Other places visited were Llandarog,' Golden Grove, and Llanarthney, which had no Mission Halls. The non-Pentecostal groups quietly set aside their much-loved 'Hymnau o Fawl' in favour of the English version 'Hymns of Praise.'

4 *Stirring Events in Llanelli*

At the peak point in Llanelli churches' post-revival development there were five churches and chapels committed to the new experience, the 'New Life.' Four out of the five were still using the Welsh language and its beautiful hymns. Nevertheless there were tensions and divisions and generation clashes. One result was that, by 1919, one could see a network of independent mission halls stretching from Burry Port in the west to Binea in the east. There was the usual division between the independent Evangelical Mission Halls, the brethren-style Assemblies and the Apostolic churches. We will examine examples of each.

Island House

A very interesting building stood in the old harbour. It was rumoured to be the work of a Quaker group. It was not far from the William Pierce fruit warehouse in which the 'Elim' Apostolic was later launched. Island House became known as the 'Place of the Vision.' Not unnaturally, I asked Mrs. Davies, "What vision?" and she said it was when a large number of worshippers saw an image on the wall of Christ in pain. It was this Mrs. Davies who was my chief informant although she spent some time away in the Birchgrove Mission. She told me,

> "The Hall was very simple and plain with no frills. We had no specialized meetings for youngsters. An excellent Sunday afternoon was spent with some singing. I know nothing about church management and finance, but someone kept proper accounts, unlike some other Mission Halls. The Creed was written within the membership's group book of names."

With the permission of the author, Mr. Cartwright, I have entered at this point another account of this strange visionary experience in 1914.

"On the first Sunday in July, 1914, there occurred one of the most remarkable incidents during Stephen Jeffreys' ministry. He was preaching on the text in Philippians 3. 10. "That I may know Him and the Power of His Resurrection and the Fellowship of His Suffering." He was aware of a special anointing upon his ministry. When he concluded his message, his wife beckoned to him to come to where she was sitting.

"On the wall, just behind where he had been preaching, and a little to his right, there appeared a remarkable picture. At first there was no clear outline, but, as he went on, a clear outline of the face of a lamb began to appear on the wall. This was clearly seen by many of the congregation. Several of the people went up to examine the wall. A man suggested that it had been caused by reflection of the electric light. But he was answered when the Pastor had the lights extinguished and the picture was still visible.

"After a time it changed to the appearance of Christ as the Man of Sorrows. The vision remained on the wall for some six hours all told, where it was seen by some hundreds of people. A photograph was taken and appeared in the Mercury and Star."

On the last Sunday in July, Stephen Jeffreys preached on the text, Matthew 24, v.8, "This is the Beginning of Sorrows." Before that week was out, the First World War commenced, as did five years of sorrow, pain and suffering.

Ty Gwyn

An old and very fruitful apostolic fellowship was started on 21st. January 1917, by those who had worshipped in a little shop in Copperworks Road, New Dock, Llanelli. They moved to a little hall under the cinema and then to Aeron Hall, where a Mrs. Jenkins kept lodgings for railway travellers. It had been signally blessed in its first pastors such as William Williams. Ty Gwyn itself had been purchased, early in 1919. Once again, our chief informant about this Hall was Mrs. May Davies who has been there for many years. Though some veteran converts of the Revival came down from Llanon, the rise and growth of this Mission Hall had much to do with great 'times of refreshing' in and around Felinfoel where Pastor Dan

(Rev. Daniel P. Williams) made such an impact in the last years of the 'tribulation' war.

This is the story that Mrs. Davies told: -

"Our Pastor was Mr. Williams. We never sought to affiliate with other Churches such as Elim. There was a Mr. Bowen, who was ordained. He went out to Irish service and then overseas. So did Pastor William Phillips who spent years in Northern Ireland. After him there was Pastor Tom Williams and Overseer, Thomas Charles.

"We did not start it because of a quarrel or a split from anywhere, but we had new helpers from other churches. At first it was a smallish, often overcrowded church with plain pews and an equally plain Communion Table on which there stood one cup and one plate. All events took place in one room, apart from the use of the tea room for Sunday school classes. The old Baptistry still remains. All members were expected to attend the Bible Class, which had a roll of 50. I can remember one Bible Teacher called Pastor George. The hymnbook was 'Redemption Hymnal' and music was upon the organ only. I cannot remember a Membership Roll to sign nor any statement of faith to learn, but I can remember the right 'Hand of Fellowship.' I had the honour of taking around the offering box, which had a long handle and a velvet lining. From time to time there was a missionary offering. Besides the two already mentioned there have been other missionaries. John Roderick Davies (Brazil) was admired and supported."

Asked about any personalities, who visited Ty Gwyn, she described Pastor Dan very accurately and said that he looked like a foreigner. Another visitor was Pastor William Phillips. In and around 1927, Lambert Jenkins retired from his ship and after three months rest at Aeron Hall he felt that God was calling him to the ministry. He was finally approved as a Pastor when he attended the Penygroes Conference and was duly anointed, probably in 1930. He was assigned to help the Jeffreys brothers. Next, he was called to a series of brief pastorates. He retired from his English pastorates in 1960. He served as an auxiliary or supplementary "evangelist" until his seventieth year. His last message was, "May the Lord visit us again with His Holy Spirit as He has promised!"

Evangelistic Hall, Arthur Street

Here we have an account by an elder - Mr. Board aged 83.

"This Hall was completely independent and has never been approached by any large movement. It had to change its title when it moved from a building known as Custom House Bank. It was solely the work of David E. Jones, who had been a field missionary in the North of England, followed by six years mission work in Tredegar. In 1882, he reached Llanelli and preached in the Wooden Theatre with the result that they had numerous weekday meetings. In 1884, he returned permanently to Llanelli and announced that he was settling at the Custom House Bank. From that austere building they moved on to Robinson Street. He was so busy that he took his recreation on the nearest beaches of the Morfa, and there he met souls who were seeking Christ. Open-air services were conducted outside the Custom House Bank and brought in many enquirers."

Of course that first meeting-place was very basic. Fifty or sixty people sat on plain seats or on backless benches. There was no prospect of a full-size Sunday school room or any other separate room on that site. Instead of Band of Hope and Christian Endeavour they had to provide something of their own. Some of the young people could take open part. They had their Bible Study schemes and their own Hymnbook called "Hymns of Light and Love," but they had no musical instruments until 1896. One other refinement after moving to Robinson Street was a proper communion table on which stood the dish of bread and two goblets of wine. Adult baptisms were performed at the Slip, the entrance to North Dock, when the tide was suitable. Pastor Jones continued his work as a cobbler but he died in December, 1907, after being granted his dearest wish - to "See the Lord send Revival before He takes me home." Before Revival reached Llanelli he took teams of witness to Southern Ireland - a risky venture. But once Revival broke out in the town he so loved, he was at its heart and kept in touch with Evan Roberts. Still later, there were fruitful meetings with R. B. Jones the great Bible teacher.

During the Revival there were some notable conversions - such as Brother Tom Pitt and Brother Tom Phillips who became witnesses throughout the rest of their lives. One of them was almost arrested on suspicion of poaching until it was seen that he only had a Bible bulging under his armpit. Other names from that fruitful time were three future overseers, Thomas Bowen, Albert Drew, the fishmonger, and William Samuel.

By the 'twenties' this fellowship was strong enough to bear the cost of building a Hall in Arthur Street - a portable building brought in sections by John Laing's workmen. This fellowship had no published records of giving but it did have a Membership Roll. The men shared the ministry. The members were well instructed in their doctrinal position and they had a proper written statement of belief. It made no room at all for spiritual activities led by Christian women. "Our women know their place." That aspect of Revival liberty was stone dead. In this respect they reacted just like Aberporth where David Jones told us how the women's praises were stopped and the Revival prayer meeting placed under a minister. As always, the numbers slowly shrank but this may be a penalty for neglecting the new truths, revealed by the Revival. They never slackened the church rules, kept a close eye on each other and would never send a member off to a new fellowship without equipping him with a commendation card. There was a special box for faithful missionary support.

Bynea Mission

This stands on or near the road leading from Llanelli to the great causeway and bridges, which link Dyfed with the Glamorgan steel and coal mine towns. Instead of travelling all the way to the Evangelistic Hall in Arthur Street, they held a weekly Bible class that flourished. They used the same Bible Reading system and the same music books as the parent church - together with a new book entitled 'Hymnau o Fawl' (Ammanford). Over the years, the Bynea mission has sown more seed in Llwynhendy where it now has its own Hall. Few details have survived and it may not have enjoyed the same success as the Apostolics. The 'twice born' people had built a place by their own labour and opened their Hall in 1917. With the assistance of Mr. John Laing they transported a complete prefabricated hall from Bristol. There was a public opening with noted guest speakers and a warm tribute was paid to Mr. and Mrs. Evans of Bynea who had given so much to the new cause and had sacrificed their home comfort also.

Every incident, including winter baptisms, was recorded in the local press and this became a kind of witness in that neighbourhood. After all, were they not committed to a 'ministry of Power and Light?' Despite its restrictive rules and small numbers, the Bynea vision and works continued. Good workers such as Mr. Strode and Mrs. Lizzie Ward came to help them. They in turn sent out missionaries such as Aneurin Ward and the Havards. They became an acceptable part of the community, having a reputation for practical kindness.

There is a very remarkable story of a gypsy encampment not far from Bynea, which was visited regularly by members of the Mission. It was a cross between a Sunday school class and a counselling discussion group. One day the camp was silent with deep grief and Mr. Evans discovered that a little gypsy lad named Billie Ford had been fatally injured in a road accident. He stood by the boy's bed side several times with the father. As the boy's life faded, other mission members came there to sing, "Pass me not O gentle Saviour, hear my humble cry." The father now broke down in total confusion and said he didn't know how to find a burial place for his little son." Mr. Evans looked at his wife and said at once -"We have a little grave in which our two dear little girls lie. You can put him to rest in there." And that is why, after all these years, you can see a little cross there with the inscription:- Billie Ford.

In the magazine 'Echoes of Service' we have this report about Bynea.

> "The numbers dwindle but the work goes on! May it continue to the day of the great visitation when everything shall be restored and ransomed and placed under Christ's rule."

Bryn or Emmanuel

There was another Mission Hall in an estate, which lies West of the river Loughor. It seemed in a flourishing condition thirty years ago, when the writer met Tom and Maggie Williams and saw their zeal for the Lord. It stood up higher on the hill than the others and could be the Penybryn, mentioned in other documents. It kept its independent status, but it established close links with Porth Bible Training Institute and was able to give practical assistance when four students took a Gospel Van around rural Dyfed.

Pencoed, to the west of Dafen

This little cause was given a site on the Stepney estate and was erected near the shaft of John Davies' disused colliery. They worshipped in full freedom and witnessed with modest success. This happened before they felt bound to divide. The extrovert and somewhat undisciplined members stayed on until they went to Ty Gwyn Hall. Those who wanted solid Bible exposition went to Llwynhendy Gospel Hall.

Llwynhendy Apostolic

This appears on the 'Showers of Blessing' list for 1912. With the help of wonderful visionary speakers, they slowly built up resources until they could open a temple called Zion. Pastor Omri Jones testified, in 1933, that there had been a little worship group meeting in Clifton House. Jones and William Thomas had been witnessing to the 'elderly poor' even before 1911. But about that time there was a great influx of 'Children of the Revival' who had been praising and magnifying God in their homes before they were baptised of the Spirit. Some of these came from Pencoed where they failed to agree on what was permissible and what was desirable and enjoyable in worship times. In the front and middle rooms of the house, in the passage and on the staircase, people were praising and prophesying. Omri Jones and Brother Richards of Felinfoel began healing. The assembly chose an Overseer, Elders and Deacons who obtained the use of the Council Schools.

Gradually there were two developments: a linkup with the mainstream Apostolics through W. Jones Williams and a quickening in public evil-speaking and scoffing, directed against them.

> "We were made to realize that God had a special purpose in view. The deep consciousness of God's presence in the midst served to mould fashioned-fine souls, and holiness in the life became prevalent. The gainsayers' mouths were shut and the Lord added to the church continually. The culmination of events was the opening of a Hall called Zion."

Another 'Echoes of Grace' report describes the opening day in the autumn of 1918 as a day of ministry from the Lord's servants who declared the heavenly vision with power and light.

Llwynhendy Gospel hall

This was set up for the sake of a remnant from Pencoed plus converts from other Halls such as Tygwyn, who desired quietness and holiness more than liveliness. This Hall has provided faithful Bible ministry for two generations. It was a beautiful wooden hut, built by members, subscribed for by Arthur Street and Bynea leaders, in order to serve the needs of a large housing estate.

Berachah, Dafen

During this period the active members also planted a new work in Dafen at the home of Elder William Richards. As usual the members saved up for a Hall which they dedicated as 'Berachah.' The preachers were Pastor Dan, William Phillips, Mr. Evans and Mr. Wilkins of Crosshands. They converted an ex-army hut into an attractive sanctuary, using voluntary labour. The first pastor's name was T.V. Lewis. During the inaugural service in their ex-army hut, now lovingly reconstructed, one evangelist rather tactlessly described the Hut as "like the Tabernacle in the Wilderness, with that repulsive badger skin outer veil, but with such beauty within." The remark was not appreciated!

Two of the leading members went off on a Mission to Ireland but at the same time the Bynea and Berachah people were coming over to develop the work in a hired place between Llanelli and Swansea. The two groups at Llwynhendy and the one at Berachah were agreed in their vision of the need of a new work there. They were able to pray together 'in one mind.'

Now that we have taken a good cross-section of the post revival witness in Llanelli, we can take the next three or four valleys, beginning with the Loughor valley which comes down from the moors to the south of the Towy.

5 *Loughor Valley, Independent Missions*

This district could vie with the Tawe valley, the Llynfi Valley and the Cynon valley in South Wales as a dynamic centre for the after-years of the Revival. Loughor and Gorseinon are the places where the 1905 Revival transformed entire communities and presented a great challenge to the elegant chapels with their highly respectable, sober and unimaginative members. In these people the Fire of Revival soon turned into glowing ashes as the converts failed to see the urgent needs of work mates, neighbours and even close families, and avoided the task of witnessing to them. This factor alone would have made it more necessary for the dedicated soul-seekers to form their own Missions. They established these, whenever possible, in the kind of zinc and wood structures built in a Bristol yard (about twenty can still be seen in the valleys). These people were joined by men and women who longed for more holiness and those who were upset about the undermining of the Word of God in many a pulpit.

In Ammanford, the enthusiasts were classified as 'pobl y sicrwydd' (assurance people) because of the strong influence of the Rev. Nantlais Williams and Mr. William Herbert's teaching. In Loughor they were better known as the 'Twice-born;' further east as 'Second Comers.' Twenty years after the Revival these groups in the Loughor valley were in a fluid state - some flourishing and some declining. Miss J. Hughes, already in her late seventies at the Golden Jubilee commemoration in Moriah, Loughor, recalled the many occasions when a group of converts would share their experiences and pray fervently for another Revival. We know of a prayer group in the period – 1928-1932, which enriched Moriah's prayer meeting. They also met in the upper room above the Post Office in Gorseinon in order to go more deeply into spiritual things.

A few hazy references suggest something like this at Hendy, near Pontardulais, which never gave birth to a Mission Hall. The high spot of the year, literally, was 'Cyfarfod y Mynydd,' a full day of praying and praising. The Rev. Daniel Jones said this meeting was held in mid-June on the slopes of a mountain at the edge of a lake - facing over to Llannon. It was started by nine people and was entirely unplanned. All day long they prayed and prepared before the opening service at 'Bethel' where 'The Lord was exalted on high.' The early morning session on the mountain began under a smiling sun.

"That was the most divine of services I have ever been in," he said. "I went into a Mount of Transfiguration in truth and we could say, 'Let us go to the mountain above - into the cloud of light, so that our countenance shall shine and all Israel shall be amazed.'"

Many of the moods and methods found on the Mountain could be seen from 1909 onwards, reflected in the Pentecostal and non-Pentecostal worship meetings. About twenty years later, a Mr. A.S. Rogers testified that he had visited many of the Gospel Halls and Missions in Glamorgan and Carmarthenshire and had found,

"The vast majority of the saints were the fruit of the Revival. The fire, kindled at that time, continues to glow like a flame in their hearts despite every effort of man and devil to quench it. They gave a welcome to the full Gospel. All the counsels of God were received and they would not suffer one teaching which went away from God's Word."

Gorseinon

Back in the Revival years the Chapels called Brynteg, Seion and Moriah had been ablaze with fervent praise and repentance and a strong seeking after full assurance. Richard Looker was impressed with Evan Roberts' ministry but other work was being accomplished. John and Rhys Penry were captured early on and they recalled moments of high drama such as the prayer - inspired by Isaiah 40 to "blot out my wrongdoings."

Figure 5: Old Post Office at Gorseinon

Evan Roberts discouraged hotheads and this group was very serious and committed. They were reprimanded by the deacons for over-running their private pre-service sessions. Another point of tension was their request to the minister to move from the despair and failure of Romans 7, to the joyous assurance of Romans 8 - "No condemnation for those who are in Christ Jesus." The ejected members formed two Gospel Missions, Penyrheol and Bryn.

Penyrheol

> "It was in 1910 that, against our wishes, we had to split from Brynteg and form the Independent Evangelical Church at Penyrheol. One deacon threatened to slap our faces. The others made it clear that we were not wanted. We were all youngsters of course and we had problems and hostility in building the foundations of the new church. We wanted to build it on a Biblical ba-

sis – 'The Lord adds to His Church such as should be saved.' So we decided never to press or urge anyone, but to accept those who were weary of untruth. Money gifts poured in and we entered our hall, free of debt. We decided to give the offering from the first Sunday of each month to missionary work. We gave an open door to ministers who were finding it hard in their denominations - men like R.B. Jones, Keri Evans and David Evans. They asked to come to this fellowship because it was so easy to preach here."

Figure 6: Penyrheol Gospel Hall in 1963

Before Penyrheol Gospel Hall was built the believers met for fellowship at the home of the parents of John and Henry Rhys Penry.

Rhys Penry recalled that baptisms were always by immersion in a "Ffynnon Bedd" outside a chapel and was performed by deacons. The same was true of the communion service for a while because one leader always said, "It is better to take communion from a poor but godly man than from one denying Christ."

Both John and Rhys Penry say that the long tradition of basic Bible instruction began when the Rev. David Evans addressed them and asked them, "Has the Lord given you your Bible and do you desire to have it in your hearts?" "We were Biblically illiterate and someone taught our group to sing, to an ancient Welsh tune, a complete list of the books of the Bible. Some of us used R.B. Jones' "Catechisms" but later went on to the "Life of Faith " Study Scheme. As to hymns, we continued to use Revival ones, such as "Maddeuant" (forgiveness) and "Come to the Saviour right now." However in later years, our Mission turned over to English hymns after we received in some converts who wanted to worship but could not manage in any Welsh Chapel.

Figure 7: Interior of Penyrheol Mission Hall

Oswald Penry remembers that other leaders at the Hall were Ben Williams, Tom Watkins (who kept in touch with Evan Roberts) and William Richards. Mr Tommy Shepherd was responsible for the 'Ysgol Gan.' Sister Wilkins, trained at Porth Training Institute, took an active caring ministry. All members were allowed to make a contribution at a service.

This Mission had given faithful support to Overseas Mission, but had not produced many candidates over many years. Their pride and joy is "Davie," Rev. David Shepherd who has been one of Wales' finest Soul-winners for many a year.

Another missionary, remembered by Oswald, was Vivian James, who served with the EMF in Norway. Collection Boxes were placed at the back of the church for voluntary contributions to church funds and for missionary support. For many years the ministry at Christmas was led by three sisters, trained at the Porth Bible Training School. The Hall was also most active in Sunday School teaching and weekday youth work.

Bryn Hall

It is sometimes difficult to disentangle the story of Bryn Hall from that of Penyrheol because they all worshipped together at first. Rev. David Shepherd made it clear that the first workers who went down to Upper Loughor were in membership or fellowship at Penyrheol and had shared in the great ejection from denominational Churches. The Williams family donated land and helped to finance the building of this Hall. A lady told us that several years after this Mission began they had to ask the leaders at Penyrheol for about fifteen new workers. Several were needed to teach the contacts after they began work in Upper Loughor. Those who wanted still more spiritual liberty also went up there to help. One worker said that only a few converts turned up for meetings there and it was hard ground in that district. They used both an English hymnbook and the 'Trysorfa Bach.'

Miss Hughes could not recall any conventions being held at Bryn Hall but they all went up to Penyrheol when someone like R. B. Jones was guest preacher. Some used to go just to hear Mr. Richard Looker, the ex-miner who was a fine singer, and who used to sing ballads, composed by converts, such as Griffiths' 'Song of the

Tramp.' One person claimed, in 1954, that "We spent the whole time singing and testifying," but there was serious Bible Study as well. They met at the homes of Mr. Vinnicombe and Mr. Maunder, where they discussed the sermons critically.

One gets a clear impression that the Bryn Hall folk were more exuberant that the sober folk at Penyrheol and more open to change. Both Mission Halls had their characters but John Penry spoke about Howell the painter who carried around posters saying 'Saved by Grace alone' and 'Look to the Lord' and 'The Blood of Jesus overcomes.' There was also a 'Text-carrying' milkman at one time.

The tape-recorded Welsh Memoirs, arranged in 1954, have moments of reverent silence, but they also have lots of cheerful crosstalk, witty jokes and hearty laughter. Still waiting in the antechambers of Heaven, these veterans were full of the Joy of the Lord and Miss Hughes prayed with unmistakable power. Her theme, as always, was the need to go on witnessing.

The Apostolic Fellowship

The few aged residents remember that there was yet another Mission Hall, which first existed in a hired cottage. Before long, they were given permission to use the Market Hall, where many exciting events took place. Those who had been involved in, what was known as the 'old Post Office prayer meeting,' and a member, called Martin Jones, used to tell stories about healings, exorcisms and 'peculiar' prophecies. For years, the model prayers, composed by Evan Roberts, were greatly treasured and used by faithful old Revival converts. People, who were happier with a more charismatic type of meeting, also frequented this meeting. If a Hall was built, it did not last long. Martin Jones returned to Bryn Hall and became a leader there.

Usually, the more zealous Revival fellowships had no dealings with the more 'way-out' causes. This was a tragedy!

Siloam

Siloam Mission lay at the back of the main road to Pontardulais. It was deeply influenced by the spirit of Revival, yet it refused to associate with the apostolic people in Penygroes, with the Hutchinson movement, or with the Jeffries movement. It stayed autonomous.

The leaders could speak proudly of their own experiences of miracles. One year there was a special Mission by a Mr. Harrison from Australia. The crowds who came to hear him, got very annoyed when a fairground, a few hundred yards to the East of their chapel, opened up its evening cacophony, and its huge steam organ drowned out the sounds of the preacher. He stopped his address and asked all the hearers to join him to appeal to God to take action. A few minutes later the fairground machinery broke down and there was complete silence.

Even the Hall that Siloam people used, was a bit peculiar. It was originally a laundry. That is why a joke went round the town. “Sinners go to the Salvation Army to be converted and then to the ‘laundry Chapel’ to be cleansed.”

There are no lists of evangelists, pastors, missionaries etc. but we know that the founder members were a Mr. Howells and the Caldecot family who were grocers and fruiterers. There was also an anonymous but wealthy well-wisher from nearby Caersalem Chapel who tried to supply their immediate needs for as long as he could.

On one last note of sad irony, after 1930, the Chapels known as the Revival Chapels had no dealings with the three Mission Halls who, in turn, had no dealings with new movements. Was the same thing going to happen at Pontardulais and Ammanford?

Pontardulais

This town had the unwanted reputation of a triple division among the children of the Revival. A local man's "Hanes Pontardulais" summed each one up in his chapter on "Little flocks." First on the scene was a cottage fellowship in Penvidi House which was only a stone's throw from the Goppa chapel they had left a few years after the Revival. The group took footing about 1910 and moved to nearby Hendy and then back again to a site near the King's Hotel.

There they built their ‘Beulah.’ Gradually, William Hill and John Dan William shifted their orientation from the Hutchinson team towards the Welsh Apostolic movement. They definitely adopted five offices and they had much in common with the Penygroes Temple later on. These changes caused distress and splitting, but the leaders went ahead to formulate a Confession of Faith. This included Justification by Faith, Baptism by Immersion, then the Baptism of the Holy Spirit with signs and tongues, prophecy and healing the sick through anointing. Finally, they endorsed the full doctrine of the Return and Millennial Reign. Their chief teacher was William Bell, the Evangelist. Many years later, the Jeffreys family brought many of them into the Elim Foursquare Movement.

A quite separate group decided to worship in Alltrego Road and they organised their Mission, called Carmel Hall, as an Apostolic Church. They recognised Richard Willliams, Richard Lewis, David Richards, John Thomas and a man called John William who emigrated to Australia. There was also a temporary Hutchinson-type group. Lastly there was a Welsh-speaking group who met in the Salvation Army Hall in Rockfield. They were linked with the senior Evangelical Hall i.e. the older fellowship at Penygroes. They eventually built their own place called Noddfa, which stayed alive and independent until the next wave brought them up as a FIEC centre.

We know a great deal about the first Hutchinson-type group. They met in village schoolrooms in meetings that they called 'Gateway to Heaven.' It was estimated that about twenty-eight launched out into the deep as a prophet commanded and they came under Mr. Rees Evans as overseer. One of their centres was called 'Tabernacle,' perhaps in memory of the great events at Penygroes. They passed through severe struggles after Hutchinson himself arrived with his own prophetess, interpreter and scribe. They claimed they had authority to set apart John Dan Williams and W. Jones Williams to be apostles and prophets for the entire Welsh nation. It is claimed that their prophecies were circulated to Apostolic gatherings in England and Europe, and that they have been preserved in the archives of the Apostolic Church in Penygroes.

This movement promised immediate power to speak in unknown tongues and other gifts, - these prophecies being gathered into small volumes. They lived a holy disciplined life, provided they first underwent an act of consecration and separation that was called the Altar Call. Another act of dedication involved bringing in tithes and offerings for missionary work. They regarded themselves as the authentic Voice of God and Channel of the Holy Spirit. Their attitude even to fellow Pentecostals became arrogant and critical.

The main road to Ammanford takes a short cut over the mountain but there was a riverside road by the Loughor to Pantyffynnon and Bettws.

Tirydail

It is hard to imagine now how the minor villages between Llandebie and Ammanford could provide enough worshippers for two or three Mission or Gospel Halls. A surviving one today is Yscennyn Mission at the foot of the old lanes leading up to the 'castle.' There was a small Pentecostal hall (perhaps from Jeffreys' time) and another independent hall on the corner of the lanes and the main road. Both have disappeared. The only remarkable thing about this Apostolic place of witness was the retired ship's captain and travelling pastor, Lambert Jenkins, who lived in retirement nearby during the sixties and who was present at prayer and testimony meetings. He often used his personal testimony as the theme of his last addresses. Here is part of his very lengthy testimony, uttered first at Penygroes Convention but repeated in Ammanford.

> "In Maidstone I went to the meeting. The place was packed, but there was one chair at the back. There was preaching and singing and I didn't understand much but people went forward from the gallery and everywhere, through a doorway on the right. I asked a man alongside me, "Where are those people going to?" He said "They are giving their hearts to Jesus Christ." I didn't understand and he said, "Won't you give your heart to Jesus tonight?" My soul was now up for auction.
>
> "The Devil on one side was bidding for me. "I will give you the pleasures of this world. I will give you anything you want. Tell Him tomorrow. There is plenty of time." The man said. "Give your heart to Jesus tonight!" Jesus was offering Life, Peace and Pardon. That was what I wanted. I was hesitating. The man said, "Maybe, too late tomorrow." If I refused now, what would happen.
>
> "I decided for Jesus. I said, "Yes! Lord Jesus!" The power of God came upon me and up I got...... I cried and wept, when I saw the Goodness of God "that leadeth to repentance," There I repented and accepted Jesus Christ as my Saviour. When I got up and went out of that place, I was a new creature. I went upstairs to my bedroom and without lighting the candle or anything, I got down on my knees by my bedside and cried for joy. Oh! Wonderful Peace! At midnight I undressed and went to bed and, in the

darkness, the place lit up with the Glory of God. The Glory went and the darkness came back again. It was the best sleep I had had for a long, long time. I am a firm believer in predestination and I believe that, from birth, the Hand of God has been upon me and I have heard His voice on many occasions."

Mr. Jenkins then recited the story of two amazing escapes from disasters at sea, which escapes he attributed to God directly speaking to him. He concluded his testimony by saying,

"God may be speaking to people today. Alter the course of your lives. If you would only heed the Holy Spirit and cry to Jesus Christ who would save you!"

After he was saved he gave up his sea career and became an Evangelist for the Apostolic Church. "From the service of the sea to the service of my Lord," he wrote in his journal,

"Wherever I was giving my Testimony and preaching the Gospel. God was using me to bring sinners to the Cross and healing sinners' bodies. Many cases of healing I have seen. Praise God! It's the power of the name of Jesus Christ. He has given us His Name not only just as an ornament, but to use His Name. Take My Name! In the Name all the Power and Authority of Heaven! Hallelujah!"

He was never trained for the ministry but spent two years with Stephen Jeffreys before choosing the Apostolic Church Fellowship. Between then and 1931, he acted as caretaker of the Penygroes Temple and received visitors, who compared it unfavourably with the old wooden structure.

Lambert was sent to Tunstall and Longston near the Thames, renting a house in Tunstall for six years, 1932-1938. Some of these fellowships were most encouraging. He retired at 65 and gave a final testimony. He concludes, "May the Lord visit us again with His Holy Spirit as He has promised!"

Ammanford

The first work in this town was associated with the revered name of William Herbert. He was converted while working in Tasmania during the New Zealand Revival of 1884. He brought the fire back to Ammanford before the Revival. He was in business as a sawyer and had his own timber yard called 'Baltic Sawmills,' yet he was not too busy to preach on the street corners. He gathered up a few faithful disciples such as William Jones the stationmaster, Mrs. Davies the landlady and 'Eli' the expert carpenter. In order to keep his flock apart from all denominational links, they borrowed the Ivorite Hall until the Welsh Revival enlarged their numbers and their vision. Later they set up a Gospel Hall in Lloyd Street and allowed anything they once possessed to go into the trusteeship of the Apostolic Church. He was now set free from cold rigidity and was often seen talking with and helping the converts. He even encouraged a Welsh language outreach in a hut near the park.

William Herbert became an excellent Bible expositor especially on such themes as Full Assurance and Holy Living. He had tremendous unshakeable faith in the Scriptures. He was often credited with the convincing of Rev. Nantlais Williams who had not heard of Full Assurance until just after he came, as the new pastor, to Bethany. Herbert was much in demand at other new fellowships such as Llandebie and Cross Hands.

It will be useful to quote the late Mr. Olwyn Jones' tribute.

> "Quite a number of the Lord's people who were saved during the Revival of 1904 had reason to thank God for the way in which he led them from bondage to liberty."

Another witness tells how habitual it was for him to shout, "To the Law and the Gospel" whenever a dispute arose. He certainly left a strong influence.

Glanamman

Details are very sketchy but Meurig Thomas could remember a Tin Mission Hall in Glanamman, run by a Mr. Owen. He was told that the atmosphere grew far too tense as time went on and the mission was eventually broken up, the members going down to the town of Ammanford. Perhaps a few went up to Brynamman (now also closed), where a group received instruction from the Revival onwards.

Brynamman Gospel Hall

High in the hills above Ammanford was a grey stoned village

where two faithful revival converts, John and Mary Lewis, began their witness. They were interviewed over thirty years ago, sitting huddled over a fine coal-fire in their pint sized kitchen. This is their testimony:

> "We, converts, at first worshipped at Gibeah but soon we wished to break away and have a Gospel Hall under the auspices of the one at Ammanford, whose leader, Mr. Herbert, had helped and guided us so often because of his unshakeable faith in the promises of God. This building, which was our vision, became possible after Missions by Matthews and Tranter. One of the leaders was John Jones of Pantycelyn, who had been an early convert in the Revival. He had been a deacon and secretary of Gibeah and also a very fine Sunday school teacher. Another leader was John Howells, the brother of Rees Howells, who was not only a deacon but an experienced Christian Endeavour leader. Every Christmas and Easter there came to this little group one of the members of the Revival Bible Teaching team, such as R.B. and W.S Jones and Keri Evans who would deal with difficult scriptures and leave the outworkings to us afterwards."

A Mrs. Thomas of Brynamman confirmed all this and testified that further instruction was given at a Young People's fellowship. Ioan Thomas of Glanrhyd added that they were skilled at presenting profound ideas like crucifying 'self,' or the favourite convention theme of the Second Coming. Mrs. Thomas noticed that whereas W.S. Jones would slowly unfold the meaning of one passage of scripture, R. B. Jones tended to put together a number of short passages relating to his main subject, and often leave printed notes with them. Some people called it the "string of beads." Another witness said that they were astounded by the humility of these princely preachers who would stop and explain such ideas as 'crucifying self' or 'the Lord's Return,' to an illiterate grandmother. Now the last living witness has gone and the Hall is closed after seventy years work. Visitors cannot forget the simple godliness of aged saints who had kept the witness pure.

6 *The Halls in the Tawe Valley*

An entire line of Mission Halls stretched down this once populous Tawe valley, from Cwmtwrch and Ystradgynlais through Glanrhyd's river junction and down past Ystalyfera and Pontardawe to the eight Halls clustered in the Morriston area.

Tro'r Glien Mission, Cwmtwrch

Cwmtwrch is sited on a tributary of the Tawe but seems closer in its relationship with fellowships to the West and South. It came into being as a response to an urgent need. George Griffiths and other Cwmtwrch Christians had noticed the ill-dressed and neglected children of the riverside district and had started a class for them. The parents asked shyly for a class for themselves so more workers went down to help.

Soon a church meeting resolved that the workers must be censured for neglecting their parent church. They were to be expelled, they said, if they did not return to the fold. George Griffiths and his helpers realised that a choice had to be made, but without offending or being offended by those who didn't understand this urge to testify to others. Outside the chapel there were acid remarks about their youth and unfitness and about their lack of a qualified minister. Criticism and scorn have long since died away as numbers multiplied and lives were blessed. The community calmed down, and the Lord sent them mighty preachers such as the Jeffreys brothers.

Stephen and George Jeffreys had entered the ministry in unorthodox ways and it was his brother who persuaded the little Cwmtwrch Mission that Stephen would be more suitable. A short Mission proved this because it was changed from one to three and then seven days as convicted sinners poured in. The next phase of the Mission lasted seven weeks and the Life of Faith called it 'Wales in the Dawn of New Revival.' Humble Stephen returned from his evangelistic tour to his flock at Cwmtwrch for a few more years and that Mission bears the stamp of his spiritual personality. For a while he was put in charge of a historic chapel - Island House, Llanelli, the place of the Vision.

George Griffiths served faithfully for another fifty years as overseer and then Pastor and has been followed by other gifted leaders. There have been further times of blessing which looked like revival - for example, in about 1956, when we saw wonderful things happening in that little hall. It was a privilege and a joy to watch young people, filled with the Spirit, become 'new' witnesses. From that crop given by the great Husbandman have come a fine Christian headmaster, a fine lay preacher, a missionary leader and a very dedicated pastor. The work was independent and Biblically orientated.

Crynant, Ystradgynlais and Seven Sisters

Ystradgynlais does not appear on any official list until after the Jeffreys campaigns in 1921-1922. Oddly enough, their Hall was called Elim Mission long before the denominational title of Elim Four Square was adopted. One pastor was a man of vision called John Jenkins of Ynys, who was ostracised, because of his testimony. His frequent absences from the coalface and his habit of praying at unusual times annoyed fellow workmen. The undermanager was told "You must go and rebuke Johnny!" but he failed to make contact because once again Johnny was on his knees.

Pastor Sparkes' group appears to have helped Crynant rather than Seven Sisters and Ystradgynlais in their formative years. It is very interesting to see that the Apostolic Church of Wales had got there first, for their magazine 'Showers of Blessing' lists a Mr. E. Jones as the overseer.

Glanrhyd

Here the Tawe stream leaves its Breconshire mountains and plunges down wooded ravines to Abercrave. A much broader valley begins to open up and Ystradgynlais straddles it. Across the Glamorgan boundary the first Mission Hall would be Glanrhyd. The story of the founding of Glanrhyd Mission is quite remarkable. It is the story of a man who had a vision from the Lord, compelling him to go and preach in certain public places, just as William Herbert had done in Ammanford, and Edward Wilkins in Crosshands. This man was Mr. Holt who was a fellow convert of the Revival with George Griffiths. He was involved in children's outreach work in Cwmtwrch, but he lived further down the valley. When adults came out in the streets to hear him, he retreated twice, like Jonah. The third time he began to preach the good news of Jesus to passers-by as well as to crowds of children.

One day in 1911 he was shown where God wanted him to use a builders' hut where the 'The Sword and Dagger' had been demolished (now the Constitutional Club.) At first he walked down from Cwmtwrch, gathering up children to his little Sunday school. Revival converts joined him in the worship and soon there were enough helpers to commence a proper Sunday school. Mr. David Meadows remembers that he used to take sandwiches with him and ate them up on the mountainside before he began his private time of prayer. In those days playing cards and gambling on a Sunday were never heard of, but Mr. Holt came suddenly upon a group of men playing cards in a hollow. He warned them about breaking the Commandment and suddenly a branch of a healthy tree cracked off, fell on top of the cards and the men scattered. Years later one of the men told him that he never played cards again.

The Baptist Union wanted to take over this new work but Mr. Holt felt it should be quite independent. He approached Colonel Gough who refused to let them have any ground for a 'despised' tin hut. A plot of land became vacant because licence for a pub had been refused. Instead, the believers acquired a mainroad hall and called it Eglwys Duw - a handsome building. Mr. Holt was led of the Lord to a builder's yard in Swansea, whose manager gave him a load of 'American pitchpine' for pews for their church. It had quite a formal layout within. It had a proper pulpit, altar and pews. On the walls there were scripture verses in place of pictures. e.g. "Worship the Lord in the Beauty of Holiness."

They used 'Redemption Songs' as their hymnbook. Offerings were not collected but placed in a box near the door. They were very scrupulous about recording gifts. At first the women had liberty but this was cut down and many regarded the Glanrhyd "Eglwys Duw" as Brethren in style. Yet we know that several women spoke publicly on Sundays and weeknights.

Suddenly there was a severe testing of their faith. The Council had sold acres of land, around the hut area, to a developer, who intended to set up a racetrack for speed races. They saw that there would be plenty of noise, dirt, bad language and gambling so close to them. So, they resolved to pray to the Lord that He would prevent this. The shining concrete tracks were laid in the spring and the next stage was about to begin when, suddenly, in June, there was a totally abnormal and unforeseen week of hard frosts. The tracks broke into splinters and the developer withdrew in despair. So the Glanrhyd Gospel Hall rose up to continue the witness. That was not the end of the story. About twenty years later the Council built a housing estate on the rest of the land and the members found that there were new families coming to join them and children coming to their Sunday school.

It was because of coldness and division among the attendees that the work went down over the years especially after Mr. Holt went off to England.

Ystalyfera

Older folk remember a mission in Godregraig, which had to be demolished along with streets of houses when the mountain started moving above them. Whereas Glanrhyd accepted anyone who professed full belief in Christ, Ystalyfera and other fellowships stayed rather close and selective in nature.

This village became the scene of a historic moment in the story of the Apostolic Church of Wales. An 'Echoes of Grace' report shows how local conference leaders went out of their way to draw in independent Pentecostalist groups by worshipping and fellowshipping together and then matching their doctrines and experiences. Only a year or two later they would unite and accept the leadership of someone like William Lewis who was assisted by an overseer, at least two elders. Any new centre was put in the charge of a new deacon.

Pontardawe

From Ystalyfera there came a fine missionary teacher named John Thomas Morris to help this little cause. Another gifted person was Griff George who could sing beautifully and could practice healing. Eventually he acted as the pastor of a Mission near Ystalyfera and he pioneered a children's work with Tal Evans. This was the work that moved to Lower Godregraig and formed part of the Peniel Mission under the ministry of Harry Price until the early seventies when he died. It is said that the Pontardawe work had begun when Pastor James and five others were expelled, not long after the Revival. In an unusual meeting, a woman had been commanded to lay hands on those seeking to be filled with the Spirit. The 'gift of tongues' was to be demonstrated later. Once the healings and the prophesyings began, there was fierce opposition but then a large group came from the Birchgrove Fellowship and were all "baptised with the Spirit who gave them power to speak in other nations' tongues and to magnify the Lord in 'another tongue.'" Few now remember Rees Morgan who went through every street singing the Gospel story, so that everyone should hear the Good News and come to the Saviour. Seven were baptised in one year.

The Green, Llansamlet

The followers, who lived in Skewen and had helped those who had bought Salem, were privileged to propagate another cause at Llansamlet. For a while, it was all put under the supervision of Pastor J.J. Williams, who was the apostle of a large district, along with his overseers.

Pentremalwyd

Still operating as an Assemblies of God Mission, it was founded as a consequence of a stirring campaign, conducted by Evangelist Stephen Jeffreys in the Forward Movement Hall in Woodfield Street, Morriston. A Swansea evening paper reported that there were miracles in those meetings, conducted by a little coalminer, "full of eloquence, not scholarship."

All the converts were called Pentecostals. Of these, 60 or 70 continued to worship together. At last, in 1923, they could afford to erect a simple wood and zinc Hall valued at £200. After 20 years in this windswept estuary, the Hall was already leaking and was far too limited for their Mission Work. No plan could be carried out while the city was being bombed and when the nearby chemical works and nickel works were a threat to safety. However a number of practical details were already catered for by the War's end. Harry Owen made plans for a Hall, a spacious vestry and a Minister's room, approved by Swansea Planning Authority. Older men volunteered for trench digging, soil removal, bricklaying and floor shuttering. The pastor worked humbly with Idwal Carter of Brynhyfryd, who was eventually chosen to do all the expert work. It took 5 years (1948-51) to complete the changeover to a purpose-built Church on the West Side of Morriston Hill.

A fine body of elders, such as W.I. Morgan, had assisted the Pastors to steer this Mission through the Great Depression. Now their post-war successors brought them through the Cold War years.

The closer to Swansea we come, the more complex will be the pattern of the Halls. There were three kinds - Independent, Brethren style and Pentecostalist. It was in this area that one could find the sharpest divisions. Recently, I have been sent a list of Morriston Halls - Wychtree Street, now demolished, Martin Street, which is no longer in use, Salem in Nixon Terrace, which is under the auspices of the Bible College and Field Terrace Mission, which never rose above its beginnings as a children's mission.

The Old Bridge Mission Hall

Situated right on the Swansea-Morriston boundary, this old hall that once belonged to a Welsh chapel, was reused by revival converts who planned various types of open-air work. A few years later, Oscar Snelling staffed it and made it an Open Mission. Anyone who attended 'the Lord's Table,' whether immersed or not, was welcome to serve there. Later again the people who founded Pentremalwyd at the top of Morriston hill borrowed the building. The Hall was often borrowed for special missions but it became irreparable by 1925. (Note. It has now been put back into use)

Figure 8: Open Air Preaching Station

7 *Many Ways of Salvation: The Swansea Missions*

This chapter should begin with a pre-revival mission of mercy. This city was host to a variety of Mission Halls, each of which was coloured by its origins, initial visions and developing aims. However, we will begin with one Mission that had nothing to do with local or national Revivals

Swansea Gospel Mission

The Gospel Mission first supported the Ragged School Work until Oscar Snelling arrived with his band of helpers and used large chambers as a 'Place of Healing.' People came there for healing and counselling. Everything else was informal. The sponsors were persuaded to engage in bolder ventures. For example, they booked the Royal Theatre for evangelistic meetings for seven years and then they had to move to the Albert Hall, which was filled every day with responsive people. It seems that the high spot of each year was the Watchnight service when hundreds responded in an act of confession.

At the start of the twentieth century, the Mission became far more absorbed in social problems. Mr. Snelling was never short of helpers and seemed able to communicate his own sunny spirit to his teams. He was always heard humming, "Be Glad in the Lord and rejoice," whilst engaged on town Crusades.

It would seem that evangelistic Missions and God-given Revivals can complement one another but can never be mixed up. Therefore, the great National Revival of 1904-5 scarcely touched Town Missions like Snelling's in Swansea, but transformed little causes.

Bethel, Mount Pleasant

Evan Roberts' close friends, David Lloyd and E.R. Lloyd formed this first Revival Mission. In their small newly built Mission Hall they saw no less than 150 people giving their lives over to Christ - of whom a percentage remained in their first churches. There is a lively picture in the local press of the townsfolk passing by the many hotels and entering into the Mission Hall. It seems that instead of being pleased that notorious ruffians were being converted, the publicans complained loudly that they were losing their livelihood because their licensed houses were empty. Ordinary people became lifelong disciples and could be heard in open-air meetings and missions, still praising the Lord after many years. The Lloyds watched with amazement as people were 'running into the nets.'

Some time after this outpouring, more Mission Halls sprang up in Swansea and Morriston whilst old Mission Halls received the kiss of life. Evan Roberts loved to watch brazen sinners, bending like sheaves. Looking down from the houses on Mount Pleasant, whenever he lodged there with the Lloyds, he would pray all night, - pleading for the people of Swansea. All round that hill, Mission Halls were being erected between 1910 and 1925, including Brynhyfryd, Manselton and Landore on the West Side of the Tawe.

Blackpill and Oystermouth

The Blackpill hall is on the side of the Mumbles Road opposite the old tramcar stop. It may be identical with a Mission, which was supported by the Glyn Vivian Miners' Mission Trust. It has not been forgotten that, for several years, students from the nearby Bible College of Wales helped its services.

The Oystermouth Hall can only be remembered by Mr. Russell of Birkenhead, who was married there, sixty years ago. It is not listed in the Assemblies of God, or in the Apostolic Church of Wales's records. Mr. Russell believes that the fellowship used a little Hall just below the castle.

Armyn Street, Fforestfach (Gurnos)

The late Meurig Thomas said that converts who had formerly attended Calvaria and other traditional chapels started this hall. One leader was Daniel Roberts who long ago had seen how an old-fashioned chapel would handle confessions of sin and error. He preferred to keep peace and harmony. Another leading figure was John Rees of Waunarlwyd who was revered as their hospital visitor as well as being their Bible-teacher. A shopkeeper, John Agadou from the China shop, Gorseinon, came out frequently to help. Other founder members were Matthews and John Denton who had a vision of a Free Mission for converts. The sole surviving founder member, Mr. Roberts aged 92, was able to outline to us the first happy days of this Mission.

> "It was filled with zeal for the Lord, men and women, witnessing together. Then there entered in the dividers - three leading men who demanded weekly breaking of bread and a larger group who said it was unscriptural for women to speak when in church. One can well imagine the distressing scenes in our homes where the husband accepted the Brethren style of service. In the interests of spiritual freedom some went elsewhere. One certain result of this division was the weakening of the witness to the new estates, built above us.

About twenty years later there was a new movement of the Spirit in the Swansea-Llanelli area. Many a rough diamond was converted at that time. One of the Fforestfach members, John Griffiths, wrote a ballad about salvation, sung in both towns.

The Saved Collier's Song

Sankeys 1079. Redemption Songs. 231.

There's a word to me so dear. Jesus saves! Jesus saves!
In the pit, with Jesus near. Jesus saves! Jesus Saves!
For when darkness filled my soul and my sins were black as coal.
With His stripes He made me whole. Jesus saves! Jesus saves!

From the fear of loud pit blast. Jesus saves! Jesus saves!
From the flames and from the gas. Jesus saves! Jesus saves!
In the pit, from sins set free, Sudden death would glory be
his is why I sing with glee. Jesus saves! Jesus saves!

When the lumps of coal I've hit. Jesus saves! Jesus saves!
Grace there is to make me fit. Jesus saves! Jesus saves!
Let the coal be soft or hard, working by the day or yard
Perfect peace is my reward. Jesus saves! Jesus saves!

Mates have often on me laughed. Jesus saves! Jesus saves!
Often saying - I am daft. Jesus saves! Jesus saves!
But in spite of all their rubs and the deputy who snubs,
While I wait for empty tubs. Jesus saves! Jesus saves!

For the pitman's lowly dress. Jesus saves! Jesus saves!
There's a robe of righteousness. Jesus saves! Jesus saves!
When the pit's cap, I'll lay down, I will rise to wear a crown,
And go singing round the heavens. Jesus saves! Jesus saves!

Philip Street Mission, Manselton

Besides Revival converts and people who responded to later Gospel Missions, there was also a group of people who had left Armyn Street, Fforestfach. That happened after the parent body had voted that the women keep silence. The daughter of one lady has described how Mr. Stan Ford and his associates had come into a meeting and declared that the Bible was against the participation of women. Many had left and moved to the more generous Gors Road or the new Manselton group.

Ebenezer, Gors Road, Swansea West

In 1936, a young man named Wilfred Beale was converted after seeing the sudden death of two of his comrades, when out cycling. Six other men trusted the Lord in baptism. He remained in Mount Pleasant Church for one year and then moved to a Gospel Hall in Percy Street, later known as Primrose Street, and later still as Meadow Street. One of the Revival converts, James Griffiths, who worshipped at Armyn Street Mission Hall, felt the urge to cross over the main road and have a preaching station there. He had started in a house but soon had to arrange the building of a zinc-roofed hut which would hold sixty or more.

From 1937, it was possible to hold a full programme and a proper assembly, which soon needed a larger place. God seemed to confirm this vision when, quite suddenly, the Swansea Town Council changed its mind about building further west and followed up an alternative plan to build one thousand houses on the North side of the western route. The Christian workers saw the need to provide a centre for worship and counselling in a larger hall.

> "It was thrilling to see over two hundred children in the Gors Road Mission. These were divided into twenty-strong Bible classes that used the Redemption Hymnal, not the usual Sankeys. Sometimes we sang in Welsh in morning services, using 'Hymnau o Fawl,' compiled by William Herbert's Gospel Hall in Ammanford, with contributions from his friends, R.B.Jones and Nantlais Williams."
>
> Mr. Beale continued his account. "We never used anything but a harmonium. Our young people's meeting went in for serious instruction, rather than witnessing with joyous vitality. When we started in 1937, we had a prayer list instead of a Membership Roll, (nothing more than an entry with a verse per member.) At some point we moved from private donations to a Church Offertory. We moved from the hall, erected in 1938 to a still more spacious place, presently called Ebenezer. Our Mission has retained its complete autonomy."

It is important to remember that not all these independent Mission Halls were created by people who had withdrawn or been withdrawn from the denominational churches because they were fanatically loyal to the infallible Word of God, or because they wanted to maintain an evangelical witness.

Many overseas missionaries were supported by such Missions as Gors Road, especially if recommended by Bible College e.g. J. Davies in Argentina and two others in India. One can check that up in the 'Echoes of Service' official prayer lists, revised every year and also the list of names of missionaries on the field recited in the Missionary Convention.

The second convention per year was for Biblical Exposition. There they could meet the people from Penygroes and Ammanford, Tycroes and Maes-y Bont, even Penyrheol. Visiting Bible teachers came from Ireland and Scotland. This remarkable man, Beale, has preached in USA, Canada, Switzerland, France, Belgium and Austria. Yet, he regarded his friend Mr. Stan Ford, the converted boxer, as even more charismatic in his witness. He has written a biography, "What God hath done."

Interlude

All these little groups concentrated on soul winning not community activity. There were many other known groups who felt an urgent need to worship and praise the Lord together – 'singing psalms and hymns and spiritual songs.' A Mr. Rowlands, who visited informal groups and took notes, collected some of the hundreds of prayers, heard at meetings of Revival converts. Amidst all the standard prayers of repentance, thanksgiving, joy etc., there appeared a few which showed understanding of what this great change in personal, social and family life would lead to.

> "Permit me Lord to use lips, which formerly cursed, to praise and glorify thee."

"O God, let me have some work to do in this new contract."

Another humble soul just wants a place to speak quietly to the Lord and she is not interested in eloquent prayers in very public places. Perhaps, she was thinking of the women who wept at Jesus' feet.

> "If I cannot pray and sing, I can still mourn (Matthew 5. v. 4-6) and make complaint and God will understand my need very well after that."

For others the great blessing was in the instruction, given in their Bible Classes. John Lewis of Brynamman said that all through the winter they went like bees after honey. They heard difficult passages explained and then went home to study until the next spring Conventions, held in Gorseinon, Ammanford and Neath. It seems that Bible teachers, such as R.B.Jones and Nantlais Williams, took endless trouble to clear up difficulties.

Those returning home from the annual "Cyfarfod y Mynydd " took this unique kind of worship with them to their own Mission Halls - free, spiritual and constantly enjoyable worship.

A scholarly eye-witness, C.F. Morris, noted the change in the prayer meetings, with dozens on their feet pleading, fervent personal prayers, bold requests for answered prayers for the outcasts and hopeless. Above all there was an intense longing to see more and more new life at whatever the cost.

The third of these converts' prayers accounts for the swift development of those local fellowships that developed into Missions. These people needed fellowship to replace the company of the tavern and the races.

> "Thank you Lord for coming to the pit and saving me. Thank you also, Lord, for the society of my brothers, for some went home with me last night. What a sweet fellowship we had on the way! Thou knowest Lord! We could not part without singing, in the middle of the street, "Duw mawr y rhyfeddodau maith," Thank you dear Jesus for such a lovely change. Oh! Let me stay in your company for ever!"

Story of the Central Church

The historian Gordon Weeks has attempted to trace the story of the first Apostolic Church in Swansea Centre. It was preceded by the missions of W. Hutchinson of Bournemouth who used an old chapel built by the Rev. Gomer Lewis in Siddall Street. He was assisted by the Rev. James Brook who practised exorcism and divine healing, and who claimed that he received a divine command in February 1910, to settle at Swansea and become an Apostolic Fellowship pastor. He took over another chapel called Bellevue in Kingsway in 1911 and prospered until Pastor Dan Williams came to the district and held wonderful campaigns.

Ernest Boulter the hymnwriter replaced James Brook in 1916 and Pastor Dan's place was filled by William Phillips (married to Catherine Jones of Aberayron in 1912 and ordained in 1916.) After nineteen men broke away from the Hutchinsonian fellowship, as predicted by one of their prophets, both Phillips and Boulter resigned. We hear little about Hutchinson's churches in Wales after the great secession. Names that survive from that area are J. J. Williams and the Bidder brothers, who became missioners in Hereford and Porth.

Development was slow in Swansea until about 1920, when a conference, held at Plymouth Hall listened to Williams, Mrs. Lewis, Mrs. Nelly Hodges and Thomas Jones, who reminded them they should keep up the Welsh language as long as possible. At this conference, Brother David Jones from Penygroes became the recognised first pastor.

The church was formally instituted on Tuesday evening, March 9th, 1920 and the two messages from the Word of God promised great things. David Jones was involved with 'Echoes of Grace.' He was a natural teacher but he was succeeded in 1931 by an affable affectionate missioner called Pastor John Hewitt - who was also a part-time missioner in Ireland. Overall responsibility passed to Pastor Rowe until just before the last war. Next came retired sea captain and preacher, Lambert Jenkins who is still with us. In his day the Mission moved once more to Tontine Street near the railway station - an awkward site, approached through a low roofed passageway. Members living round Siddall Street found a better site in Alexandra Road - an Urdd building that they turned into a lovely church christened Beulah. Since then, it has moved twice and is now in St. Helen's Road.

In Swansea East, there were three Missions. Their unusual feature was that individuals with vision set up these Missions.

Bonymaen

An Anglican lady used her personal fortune to set up a zinc-roofed hut in Bonymaen. It was a single strong-floored room, which suited children's and youth work. It is disbanded now and it has been used recently as a young boxers' training booth. Yet a little wooden Cross still stands on the roof-peak.

Winchwen

About a quarter of a mile away is the well-built Winchwen Gospel Mission, which has had a chequered life. Just before the last War, Mrs. Blodwen Joseph and Mrs. Evelyn Thomas began to meet for prayer in their own sitting rooms. Gradually, other Christians joined them and someone suggested that they built their own hall. After several attempts, they were offered a site to erect a hut, which was brought over from Cefncribwr. This project has taken 30 years to reach completion with a new Hall, erected in 1967 and a Pastor. Most of its story lies outside the confines of this survey.

Birchgrove

The first Mission Hall across the Tawe Bridge, it became a separate entity in August 1917, when 'Pen Moriah' was opened. A correspondent for the magazine 'Echoes of Grace,' blessed it with a private vision in which a royal swan, on a rock, was getting ready to do battle while a kingfisher was trying to pierce a many-tentacled octopus. They sent this to the 'Prophets of Penygroes,' who interpreted this as Christ killing the sin that strangles everything. This aroused widespread attention. On the opening day of the Hall, they formally invited W.H. Lewis to be the first pastor. He was a truly saintly man.

The report ends, "We had proofs of the presence of the Lord and the sealing of the Spirit." This would be generally applicable to most of the Swansea Missions.

Landore Mission

These people found a single room in a large private house, down in the ravine between Mount Pleasant and Manselton, a place of noisy marshalling yards. This room could be partitioned and was well used by Sunday school classes and weeknight children's activities. Adults sometimes came for the occasional guest services, taken by Bible College students. Landore was known as an open-hearted fellowship, which could use the Keswick Hymnbook, the Redemption Hymnal and the Sankey's Songs and Solos, as and when they felt led. If they attended Conferences they advocated the full doctrine of the Millennium Reign and the Rapture of Saints. Its main Bible Class was led for years by Mr. Richard Fields and the nickname "Field's Mission" sticks in old folks' memories. Finances were simple, as only only two senior men recorded all gifts. An annual report was available.

The Landore Mission remained completely independent and they managed to build a wooden hall, which was later burned down. If there were a pastor he would have been "Billy" (Williams?).

8 *The Faithful Witnesses*

The chief informant for this large district, Pastor Len Sparks, confessed that although he had preached in many Mission Halls, he had not always taken close note of the surroundings, nor enquired after the membership and leadership.

Tonmawr Independent Mission

This small colliery village is situated high up above Neath and Cwmavon. The oldest chapel and Manse can be seen at the foot of dense steeply rising woods. Two groups had withdrawn from traditional chapel life and formed the Upper and Lower Missions. The Upper Mission, led by a Mr. Griffith Thomas, served a street of twenty-four families, yet it had no children's meeting. Converts had to cross a perilous viaduct, which carried the tramlines, to worship in a small hall. Another group had already formed a distinct service by 1920 and had arranged to hold a separate Prayer and Bible Class in an old shop in Blaenavon Street. As they grew, they moved on to a grocer's shop in Welsh Row. Two great events marked the first ten years. They benefited from the arrival of a group of families, which migrated from Hereford during a slump and decided to attend the Hall instead of the Anglican Church.

The second event was the coming of Louisa Thornley and Esther Thomas, sponsored by a City Mission. It was commonly claimed in that district that "Louisa knocked them down with her thunderbolts and Esther picked them up again." There were many converts so they had to move once more. They bought an old stable in Tonmawr and re-erected it on their own site. Designer concrete panels have now replaced the enlarged hut. Inside the chapel there were a hundred good seats, a pulpit, a donated communion table and a fine pipe organ - a Salter - given by generous friends. Services were very basic with hymns drawn from Sankey's collection. There was a Roll of Membership but it did not contain a Statement of Faith in any written form. All born again believers were welcome as members and the church belonged to no other organisation. Women enjoyed considerable freedom but were kept out of the pulpit, despite Mrs. Penn-Lewis' warnings. They kept to the fundamentals and the gospel was preached constantly and consistently. They produced no missionaries but they faithfully supported Missionary societies by setting aside the Monday prayer meeting collection each week.

Len Sparks had lots to say about the general witness of this Mission Hall and how they rejoiced in street witness. He says that at least once their leader, Griffith Thomas, led the mission at Upper Tonmawr into new projects. The children's meeting needed far more room. As the work grew stronger, there was increased outdoor activity, including the engraving of key salvation texts in deep white on the prominent rock outcrops. Len Sparks, Enoch Jones and John Hughes did these engravings.

The young converts had no training in Christian work and the methods of the Christian Endeavour were unknown. They rarely went to Conferences. The converts had considerable influence in their workplaces also, especially John Hughes who was once so violent a rebel that he used to try to drag his wife out of chapel meetings - until that night when certain prayers penetrated and a certain line of a chorus, "Throw out the lifeline. Someone is sinking today! " brought him to repentance. He was so outspoken that he angered people. One manager turned on him and said, "The trouble with you is that you have a slate missing." John said, "Well! Praise God, for in that gap the light came through and brought me to joy."

At least five of these sturdy believers held responsible positions in the Garth colliery. "One day the under manager walked in on me and said desperately, "Please show me somewhere in this colliery where I can swear. Wherever I go, there is one of your lot looking and listening." One unique feature in that region was the Miners' Lodge meeting which always began with prayer and which always reached agreement. They were obeying exactly the guideline laid down by Evan Roberts in a Christian newspaper, about prayer as the best solution for reconciling opposed parties.

Many years passed by before this group was renamed as the Tonmawr Free Mission, which remained independent for about 40 years. It reminds us that not all the Independent Mission Halls were created by people who sought more free and fervent worship. Some were aware of needy people around them and took steps to reach them. Some were established to protect the preaching of the True Gospel, whilst others left traditional chapels, because they wanted to reach and save their neighbours more speedily. A Rev. Rowlands, who went around collecting converts' prayers, could hear this note of urgency. "Let me, Oh Lord, continue the work of teaching children. Oh! Let them not be taken down the road of sin, which I walked in the days of my youth."

Pontrhydyfen

The only definite reference we have of a Mission work there is a brief memoir from a Gors Road veteran that their first zinc-roofed hut was redundant and was demolished and transported in order to be used as a Sunday school room. It drew in large crowds of children, among whom was Richard Burton, the actor, so they say. The 60-year-old hut could still be seen in the village until recently.

The Clyne Mission Hall

One of three linked with the Glyn Vivian Mission to miners, this Mission began life in a hut, later replaced by an old-fashioned Hall with a plain pulpit and communion-table. (This is now being rebuilt after a fire). This Mission believed in open membership being offered to those who said they had been born again. "No credo was recited, no specialised doctrines stressed and no letters of commendation were needed. But we know when all is genuine," said one witness. When Mr. Voke inspected Clyne, in March 1927, on his way to the Forest of Dean miners, he complained that, "There is a stubborn spirit there because of cold Christians. There is a need for restoration." The Sunday school went from strength to strength until it had six classes on Sunday - for ages of 3, 5, 7, 9 and 11. So the pastor's afternoon was full of activity. No fellowship was had with other missions. For some years after the depression the Clyne Mission began to recover strength. The advent of Pastor Sparks marked a significant new drive.

Figure 9: Clyne Mission Hall

Crynant

Pastor Sparks thought that many years ago he had been able to help E. Jones in a little corrugated iron hut. It is not clear how far back the Crynant branch goes. They had no links with their fellow-believers in Glynneath or Seven Sisters.

Skewen

The first reports of excitement and success come from 1917, when the highest quality open-air meetings were held in faith. The blessing moved the entire church although it was unable to meet anywhere except within homes. In its early days they had ventured to borrow Saron, which later they purchased, refurbished and cleansed. For five years they worshipped in this way until 1921. Five years later they had grown so large that they had to build a new Saron Mission Hall. The church was soon able to furnish a full complement of apostles, pastors, prophets and evangelists. “We are expecting yet more fruit from the Lord,” said one leader.

‘Echoes of Grace’ talks about a day of power and victory, which moved and strengthened the church. As at Crosshands there was a mixture of crying and loud magnifying of the name of the Lord. Loosely linked with it, was a cause which first worshipped in Copper Works Road Hall, which can be confused with one in Llanelli. Five 'Saron Hall' people also pioneered cottage fellowships at Resolven and Glynneath until the latter could afford its own assembly hall. A pastor, called Rosser, worked hard, building up the three fellowships and a fourth centre called Pen Moriah. Birchgrove (Saron Hall, 1916), was bought in circumstances which showed the power of God to open doors. It became a focal point for the fruitful work of Pastor J. Dan Williams who took his teams of witness to Aberavon, Pencoed, Maesteg, Nantyffyllon, and Pontycymmer.

Figure 10: First Lonlas Mission Hall, Llansamlet

Their first management structures and new buildings are now seventy years old. The work was consolidated and formalised by 1928, when the main Apostolic Church of Wales reached out its hand of fellowship. Seven years later they were all formally assenting to the document, ‘Fundamental of Fundamentals.' Over and over in the twenties they heard the cry arise, "Come over and help us!" The response was glad and vigorous, until the next decade, the age of Depressions and Strikes, when all our evangelical Churches, whatever their colouring, were deprived of dozens of active workers who went off to Coventry, Luton, Slough and Bristol to find work. To put it colloquially it knocked the stuffing out of the most outgoing, soul-winning Churches and left all the others to retreat into comfortable refuges.

Figure 11: Interior of Lonlas Mission Hall

This appears rather late in time, when the entire concept and practice of the Mission Halls was fast fading, making way for new forms of Holy Spirit work. This Mission came out of a heart, full of compassion and a mind full, of imaginative vision. The late Major Allister Smith followed every development in the story and he would have added more words, such as compassion, vision, watchful prayer and unshakeable faith. As a child, Mrs. Neil had been well taught in the scriptures but it was just one call of God that haunted her, "Choose ye this day whom you will serve" and "Remember now thy Creator in the days of thy youth." The final decision had to be NOW but the Now took four years. Almost the same time elapsed before she was assured that God's first plan for her life was not an overseas missionary vocation, but married partnership with Ernest Gethin Mc'Neil of Neath.

Her first concern was for little children so she set up a Sunday school in her own house and taught them the well-known miracle stories and used well-tried children's hymns. Two years later, the Lon Las Mission Hall was on the way - situated on donated land, with freely given resources and cost price-heating systems. After they had prayed the Lord sent them a skilled organist, Mr. Albert Bowen. Another gift came from the Guest Speaker and was hung behind the pulpit. "WE PREACH CHRIST CRUCIFIED." It was a successful launching and one of the last.

Neath (Cecil Street) Mission

Nothing can reflect the individualistic nature of the Mission Hall better than the story of the Cecil Street Mission, set down in the midst of the poorest and most ignorant people in that town. An aged daughter told us how her parents, Mr. and Mrs. Joan Rosser, felt that they should do something for the district, so they spent much time and energy on building a Hall. Its sole purpose was to bring lost people to the Saviour, so there was no pool for baptisms, neither was Communion served there. There was a very large Sunday School of course - three or four classes intermingling in one room. My informant was then a little girl who just stared at the old women who wore hard flat caps and heavy shawls that covered their threadbare clothing.

Because we are all new creatures in Christ you could see the gradual transformation in their language, manners and customs," said Miss Prosser. This work continued throughout her parents' lifetime. It was a shining example of soul winning through love and service.

Research has failed to uncover any other Mission Halls in the Neath Valley, until you reach Glynneath at the top. One can see the infinite variety of God's dealings with His people in the Neath area from Neath eastwards into the Anglicised district on the coast, such as Margam and Briton Ferry and there is more to be discovered.

9 *Along the Ridge to Aberkenfig*

A huge park, normally associated with Margam Abbey, forms a major break between the Kenfig Valley and the Afan Valley. As we cross over between the two, we can briefly visit that converted chapel on the Bryn, which had been bought privately by a Mr. Millichamp, who had his own vision. This was the stranger who wished to rename his chapel - Eternity so that every passer-by could be told, "We are going to Eternity Tonight! But, are you?"

Descending the Margam Woods, through old bridle paths, we can revisit an Independent Mission, called Ynysafan.

Ynysafan Gospel Mission, Cwmafan

A mile or two from Port Talbot the River Afan leaves its twelve-mile ravine and bursts between two rocks into the coastal plain. It was a sunless spot with viaducts casting deeper shadows. The big Welsh chapels here were greatly stirred up by the 1904-5 Revival, but bad mistakes were made and unwise things said and these churches went back to 'formality.' As things worsened a minority of converts sought escape, but that was not their only motivation. Several of these halls are sited in places where the new converts longed to reach lost people and bring them to the Saviour's feet.

Ynysafan Gospel Mission is our best example because it was totally independent and its root went back so far that it has a church rule in its records "that the services shall be in Welsh and English." The Mission took on board the passionate teaching of Pentecostals such as Mr. Price from Swansea but made a simple declaration in their Church Rules - "That there is no doctrine of "tongues" to be taught, preached and practised in this Mission Hall." The Independent Mission ensured that only existing officers could nominate officers who must then be appointed only by church members. These officers had to promise to obey the church rules first and foremost so there was no question of any outside pressure or deviations. They never sought integration with either the Apostolic Church in

Wales or with the much later Assemblies of God, nor with Brethren assemblies.

Special procedures were invented to deal with those who wanted to transfer membership to some other fellowship. It adopted some methods practised by Brethren but with one important distinction. It stated bluntly in its own rulebook "that sisters can be elected as officers in the proportion of three to four of the number of men appointed officers." Older eyewitnesses remembered a ruling that whoever was doing the Bible exposition from the Pulpit Bible should mark in ink the verses he was using. An amazing amount of creative imagination must have been expended in interpreting and applying certain verses. We know that some of the other Missions, such as Cross Hands, Brynamman and Bynea, sent for the famed Bible teachers such as R. B Jones when some passage of scripture confused and divided them.

How did this independent mission come into being? It is almost certain that this took place in three stages. First of all certain very sincere and serious minded people discerned in their spirits that their traditional churches were too mixed - with a sprinkling of Christadelphians and even Unitarians. As these nine pioneers, who wrote and signed the church deed, felt they must work out the doctrinal basis of their fellowship, they wrote,

> "None other than the teachings of the Trinity be preached i.e. the Fatherhood of God, the Divinity of our Saviour, Jesus Christ, and the fellowship of the Holy Spirit." (See Appendix B.)

Then a much larger group from different backgrounds came along as the result of local Missions, which brought forth a desire for sharing experiences. No-one can remember which Missioner was responsible in those early days;- Pastor Dan, Matthew Francis or David Matthews, the Welsh Evangelist. Here is a lovely picture from those days of a baptism in the coal dust laden river almost under the old bridge, which was so close to their Mission Hall. Again there is a strange feature here - the rules stipulated that they believed in baptism by immersion, yet they also permitted the sprinkling of water on babies and accepted it as some kind of baptism.

The Mission had long outgrown its first accommodation and had set up a hall. It was the usual structure, fashioned out of corrugated iron sheeting and a zinc roof, which concealed and protected the finest of wooden panelling. The hall occupied about 70 by 40 feet. Much of the interior furnishing and lath planking were the work of a local undertaker who used donations to get supplies. The Hall was proud owner of a magnificent pulpit made by him, a piece of fine craft only recently vandalised. That Hall lasted until 1992, when maintenance made too many demands on an ageing membership.

Figure 12: Baptism in the River Afan around 1924

According to Mr. and Mrs. Vaughan, there was a third even greater influx of converts round about 1922-1923, probably as an echo of the Jeffreys' campaigns, which blessed many a Mission Hall. They remember great crowds of people waiting to get in to a gathering, which was in full song and was at times a little unruly. The effects of this wave were far shallower and less enduring.

Until the last war, both Church and Sunday school exercised considerable influence on the community. Members were enjoined to live a disciplined life and seek after holiness - and this they did for two generations. But the cause moved elsewhere in 1942.

The big industrial complex known as Port Talbot and Margam must have had at least one post-revival hall, but no details have reached the author.

The High Moor

All the way from Pyle to Aberkenfig, there is a high ridge road with a chain of little villages, descending abruptly into the next valley. They overlook the river Kenfig, which has the curious habit of flowing inward from Southwest Kenfig Burrows to its Northeast confluence, Along that road, you will find three or four lively Mission Halls, including the one at Cefn cribwr. Amongst them is the large Bethlehem Pentecostal whose story has been told by D.R.J. Ollerton.

The work can be traced back to home prayer-circles, recommended by F.B.Meyer and by Mrs. Penn-Lewis, who wrote a pamphlet called 'The Revival Call to the Churches.' The first Prayer-circles were in Caersalem, Berea and Siloam. The only direct contact with Evan Roberts was at a special preaching service at Capel y Pil and this was very emotional and disorderly.

Many of the converts went to Siloam, where the Pastor D. Williams welcomed such behaviour as singing, laughing and clapping. There were open-air meetings in the woods and on the common, yet the 'Children of the Revival' longed for still more experiences of God, like that of Wales' pioneer preacher, Pastor Hill, who spent one hour in prayer each morning before he went out to preach in liberty and power. In November 1908, he left Penyfai for Calfaria in Cwmfelin, Maesteg, because he wanted a system of freewill offerings.

He had often preached of the need to experience a 'Personal Pentecost' and yet it was not until June 1910, that "The Spirit fell upon me and He spoke through me in other languages." He set up a small fellowship in the home of a Mr. Bedford, in Bridgend Road next to the Cross Inn, and their meetings were 'full of the New Wine of the Spirit.' He admired the Jeffreys brothers but threw in his lot with Pastor Hutchinson of the Apostolic Faith Movement in Bournemouth. He seems to have set up his own meetings for a year or two after being recalled to 'Smyrna.' The first disciples were the Stenners and the Phillips family.

In the twenties, he helped Pastor Dan Williams to form the Apostolic Church in Wales because it went boldly into cinemas and other places to witness He did not break off relations with Rev. D. S. Jones or Rev R. B. Jones.

When the Cefn Cribwr work began, under the leadership of Dan and David Phillips, they reached out all the way to Kenfig Hill, seeking to baptise with water and the Spirit. At some point, they adopted 'anointing with oil' for healing, usually at the home of Mrs. Phillips. Outsiders complained about imaginary experiences, such as shaking under the shock of prayer, but they saw themselves as people keeping the True Fire burning. In 1923, they were accused unfairly of 'free love' meetings, secret immorality and 'dancing in the Spirit.' Nevertheless, keener Christians joined them in the 'Cottage Ministry.' Despite occasional disagreements, the Stenner's, the Phillips's and the Matthews's came regularly to this Prayer-room. In order to hold 'Holy Ghost' meetings.

A few years after, they bought land in Cefn Road. They called their Hall, 'Bethlehem,' and they enjoyed fifteen years of fruitfulness, all along the ridge. Their finest pastor, Griff George both sang and preached the gospel for over ten years, culminating in a mini revival in 1945. He believed in and preached the imminent return of Christ. Just before the Second World War, they decided they needed an enlarged Church.

Bethlehem Pentecostal, Cefn Cribwr

The Church's historian, D.R.J. Ollerton claimed that this church originated from a prayer circle in three chapels, in response to a Keswick pamphlet, entitled 'A Revival Call to the Churches.' (F. B. Meyer.) Leading members were David Beale, Edward Stenner, Tom Francis, David John and Evan Lloyd.

Ollerton also claimed that after Evan Roberts preached at Capel y Pil, there was a great deal of uncontrolled emotion. At first, the minister of Siloam welcomed meetings, where singing, clapping and laughing were commonplace. He also encouraged open-air meetings on the Common. They wanted permission to hold midweek meetings for 'Liberty and Power.'

Meanwhile, Pastor William Hill had experienced a personal Pentecost and arranged to hold a weeknight meeting, 'Tarrying for the Baptism of the Spirit.' Pastor Hill did not leave his third church, Smyrna. Yet, he was dissatisfied after his blessing and linked up, first, with Mr. Hutchinson of the Apostolic Faith Movement, then with Pastor Dan and finally with the Jeffreys brothers. By 1923, his personal following needed its own centre and a man called Mr. Rowe from Sheffield bought Aberkenfig House, to which was added a derelict cinema. His work branched out in two ways, the most important being at Cefn Cribwr.

Figure 13: Inside of Cefn Cribwr

A man called Dan Phillips, a builder, had come home from U.S. A. and came under Pastor Hill's ministry. He and his brother and sister-in-law were soundly converted and linked up with the Stenners of Cefn Cross, who were baptised by immersion in 1921 and by the Holy Spirit in 1923. Even before they built a Hall, they were being abused and accused of having imaginary experiences. Pastor Hill's personal experiences of visions and voices were not acceptable. Others objected to his practices of 'anointing with oil for healing.'

The final development took place after a series of open-air services and the after meetings, which followed. In November 1923, a proper Assembly was formed and the villagers accused it of "free love meetings,' secret immorality and "dancing in the Spirit.' Despite this, Edward Stenner transferred from Siloam, Jennie Phillips came to accompany the singing of the Psalms, Mr. Westcott came in as a healer and Mrs. Matthews found a Prayer-room in John Street where began 10 years of cottage ministry. In 1927, they moved from Mr. Stenner's land to Cefn Road and then built Bethlehem, 'the House of Bread.' It was dedicated to the preaching and defence of the Word of God. A new pastor, Griff George, preached the Imminent Return of Christ. During its many years the Bethlehem Mission became involved in Mission support work in Bulawayo.

However, there has also been in Bethlehem's history, seasons of special and sometimes wonderful visitation. Times when Divine impressions and activity can be seen to be more intense. Cefn Cribwr's nearest neighbours were at Aberkenfig.

Beulah Mission Hall, Aberkenfig

William Hill's life could be called restless, with two pastorates in Bridgend, one in Maesteg, a part-time one in Cefn Cribwr and, finally, one in Beulah Mission Hall, Aberkenfig House. The first members of Beulah came out from Smyrna, Penyfai, from Hope, Bridgend and a few from Calfaria, Maesteg, about 50 in all.

Figure 14: Beulah, Aberkenfig

Pastor Hill believed in living by faith and would not receive a fixed salary. Instead of a fixed collection, members were told to put their offerings in two boxes, placed in the back of the hall. Under the leadership of a succession of elders, drawn from the original membership, the Mission Hall was kept in excellent condition until its vestries were acquired by the local council and then demolished. (An attractive pebbledash Hall replaced the older one in about 1980.)

Miss Loosemore is a grandchild of the Mission and she remembers that Pastor Hill occupied a building, next to the Mission Hall. The inner walls of the Mission Hall were wood-panelled and the front wall had text scrolls, such as 'It is finished,' 'I will do Marvels' and 'Only believe.' There were 21 benches, half of them upholstered. The pulpit was only a reading desk on a raised platform concealed by velvet curtains, running on wooden rails. Below the pulpit was a large chair with arms and a small chair. Then there was a large table, covered with a white communion cloth. In the times of worship, Redemption Hymnal was used on Sundays and Redemption Songs on the weeknights. There was a twin-pedal organ, which once belonged to Pastor Hill but there was no band or choir.

One special feature was the status of the women members, which was equal to the men. They had women preachers, but preferred the women to wear hats. There is no trace of a Bible Class, especially during the years when they were linked with the 'Assemblies of God' Movement. There were no strong views about personal Salvation, but a great deal of teaching about sanctification. This Hall was the Spiritual Home of Rev. Selwyn Hughes, (Every Day with Jesus), Roderick Davies (Brazil) and of Eric Dando, (the future Pastor of the Newport 'Assemblies of God').

The ten 'fat years' of joy and excitement were followed in 1932 and 1933 by ten 'lean years,' caused by disputes and ill feeling between the elders. Dan Phillips gave up his leading position and Charlie Roach was treated as a competitor rather than a helper. Their decision to join the Bible Pattern Church Fellowship ended this bad patch and led on to another ten years of great blessing during the Great War. We end with a comment from their historian,

> "For church to belittle faithfulness and regular commitment in the long months and years of 'small things,' and to expect the dramatic and sensational continually, is to misunderstand God's way with His people and give an unreal impression. All the forgotten days, acts of love, words of testimony and humdrum of church

life is often so ordinary as to be difficult, if not impossible to relate, but this history in no way wants to give the impression that such was not the case."

10 *The Heart of the Missions*

Bridgend is at one end of the Vale of Glamorgan and Barry is at the other. Between them is twenty square miles of farmlands and woodlands which appears to have been untouched by Revival influences. Therefore, our survey begins with Bridgend and the various river valleys - the Llynfi, the Garw, the Ogmore and the Kenfig. These busy industrial villages sent a first stream of coal and iron, another stream of clever, ambitious lads, and a third vital stream of spiritual enthusiasts and men of vision. At the southernmost point was a chapel or mission called Philadelphia Street, Porthcawl. At its northernmost point was Llantrisant which was the key to the Rhondda and Taff Valleys.

We shall begin in the town of Bridgend itself, that town which had been mesmerized by the dynamic mission work of D.S. Jones - better known as 'the tramps friend.' D.S. Jones could never fit precisely into any doctrinal system or movement and he worked willingly with the Salvation Army and the Catholic priests if they shared his compulsive pity for all wanderers and confused, fallen men and women. After he was virtually expelled from his denominational church, strangely named Ruamah (Mercy), because of the sometimes embarrassing results of his generous aid to 'down and outs,' he set up his own mission centre, as close as possible to the river bridge where seven roads met.

In the same town there was another minister whose methods were causing serious embarrassment in his Church. The Rev. David Evans of Hermon had appeared to be a serious and studious young man. Now he was to be seen in 1905, talking on the street corners, giving out tracts and rebuking church members for their cold loveless attitude to 'the lost.' He began his own work in the 'Upper Room' above a coach-house, but removed to what some people called the 'bottom hall.' There he trained his own student workers, managed his church affairs without deacons and opened his arms wide to others who believed in Full Assurance, in Holiness and in the soon Return of Christ and Rapture of Saints. He was always a welcome preacher/teacher at Bible Conventions yet he was humble enough to ask R.B. Jones, W.S. Jones and Nantlais Williams to come to his fellowship meetings and enrich the minds and quicken the spirits of the converts. In later years he took charge of the Faith Mission to Wales but his relations with the Mission became strained and he moved elsewhere.

A kind of Prayer Intercession Fellowship existed in Bridgend before the outbreak of the Revival. The Rev. David Evans passed on a delightful letter, in December 1905, to Jessie Penn-Lewis from Kate and Jane Leach. It shows their longings and their readiness to intercede for their district and their conviction that

> "prevailing prayer in union with our living Lord will bring down upon the town, conviction of sin. Though the powers of darkness are very real, they will become sham powers when faced, through the Blood of the Lamb."

The next much talked of development in Bridgend was the work of William Hill and his followers who found the old Penyfai chapel a little cramping. They took over the old Hollybush pub and turned it into an embryonic Pentecostal mission, dedicated on December 18th, 1907. Mr. Hill moved on to the Maesteg area but the little group picked up support from many revival converts with whom they shared prayer and bible study. The writer would hazard a guess that the original Leaches' circle joined them as they seemed to speak the same language. Both these groups had urgently needed wise leadership and it was not enough to have the occasional help from the Revs D. Jones and David Evans.

Mrs. Mary Morgan of Pen-y-fai was able to give a vivid picture of the David Evans' Mission whose proper name was Freeschool Court, because her grandparents had belonged to the breakaway group who followed David Evans. Though there were other surface reasons why this group withdrew or were excluded from Hermon, the root reason was "they wanted to go further into the things of God - to follow on from their Revival experiences."

The new Mission Hall had seating for about two hundred and had proper pews, pulpit furniture and an organ. Because of lack of space, except for a little kitchen for serving meals, the children's work was always incorporated in the main service. Mrs. Morgan was not aware that there had ever been a Membership Roll or a Foundation Deed with a Statement of Faith, nor was there a connection between it and any Missionary body or Movement. It was well-known that all contributions to the China Inland Mission were recorded carefully and the gift boxes opened on a special Missionary Day. This Mission suffered the usual fate of a rather exclusive group who chose to stay in the centre of town, instead of on one of the housing estates. Through deaths and removals the membership declined rapidly after 1940 but the faithful few held on until a new body - the FIEC - took over some fifty years ago. Mrs. Morgan paid this final compliment:

> “It was a privilege to have been brought up with them. On Easter Monday people would come down from the many valleys for open worship, testimonies and prayer. Women were not forbidden to take part in these spiritual events."

Hallelujah Hall

This could also have developed later out of a crossmatch between the Rev. David Jones, and William Hill's disciples and the Leech sisters' prayer intercession group once favoured by the Rev. David Evans. These women emphasised the full implications of the message "Jesus is Lord of All.” They prayed first and foremost for their own town, and then for the numerous villages. Their successors, down to this day, have been firm believers in prophecies, healings and other miracles, which are told, in great detail by a recent correspondent, Geoff Gray.

The ones whom I met occasionally spoke in tongues, without regard to the Biblical rule about the need to have interpreters present. An older member told us that the pre-war worshippers had been quite uninhibited and very vocal. Some enemies called them the ‘Hallelujah People’ because the original owners christened it as ‘Hallelujah.’ They have changed premises once or twice and can be found on the outskirts of Bridgend.

Litchard Mission

A wartime service was initiated when a large number of trainee camps were near and many Christian men in diverse uniforms were seen. The first meetings were not very far from a War Hospital and a prisoner-of-war camp. Then they pioneered a post-war development in the heart of a new housing estate.

They began in various rooms and centres and developed a large 'outreach.' It is certainly a purpose-built chapel hall and is cared for by members. It has built up a considerable amount of children's outreach from the new estates. It is totally independent and run by its elders. Their first minister was Eric Robinson. They have been blessed by God with a series of evangelist-pastors beginning with Hywel Griffiths, the 'preaching collier' from Tonypandy, Peter Phipps Mike Mellor, now a Covent Garden church planter in London and Jeff Marshall, evangelist.

Tondu and Nantymoel

Both the Pentecostal (Beulah) and the Gospel Halls (Brethren) arrived rather late in Bridgend town and there was little movement for many years. It was quite a different story as you walked up one of the four valleys - the Kenfig, the Llynfi, the Garw and the Ogmore/Ogwr valley. After Aberkenfig, which we have met in the western group, we come to a village called Tondu. It was here that a remarkable convert, Brother Tom exercised widespread influence, so much so that his highly spiritual letters are preserved until this day. This bully, braggart and feared bruiser was totally changed by the Grace of God and by the patient teaching of the Rev. David Evans. Disabled by lung disease in his mid-forties, Brother Tom could hardly give his testimonies in a prayer meeting, but he could write like an apostle and no-one understood how this self-taught man could be so mighty with the pen. In the twenties, he was a bridge between Mission Hall leaders and a remarkable spiritual 'Society' which had gathered at Dover under the leadership of Mrs. Beresford Baker and Miss Rogers. Here is a sample of his wonderful letters that the Rev. David Evans placed in 'Yr Efengylydd.'

> "I must tell you the great joy we are having – Heavenly! Immense! Glorious! I have been asking God the Holy Ghost to reveal and manifest Jesus and His Cross to me, and He has taken me at my word. I find the plank very narrow and I am entirely dependent on Him now, but it is beautiful pasture. I should like to tell you what my Heavenly Father is doing to me now. He is

moulding me and fashioning me and teaching me to abide in Jesus at all costs. When the principalities and powers are raging, He is teaching me the lesson - to abide. If this lesson has not been well learned, we cannot be trusted with power. When I have learned this lesson, I shall come from the Baby Class.

"I should like to point out to you that the outer worship is diminishing and everything is drying up, but the inward worship is going on in tremendous adoration. Words cannot express Glory to His Holy Name. God is speaking daily to me. I am losing the grammar fast but I am having the hidden manna. I am going to tell you a little about how I am going on, since I don't get to morning worship. I do thank our beloved Father in Christ Jesus for having made His precious word sweet. I give Him the care of waking me in the morning."

Were there any more saints of this kind in the neighbouring Mission Halls?

Maesteg (Nantyffyllon)

Brinley Richards the local historian made a fair and balanced account of different kinds of religious development in the Llynfi valley. He noted that the saintly Dean Howells of St David's cathedral had actually conducted a Llynfi Valley campaign just three years earlier. Even then the Revival fire began to flare up, but not as high as in 1904-5, in places like Nantyfyllon. That village is mentioned because Glasnant Jones, the Revival pastor, Annie and Maggie Davies, the singers, Rosina Davies, the eloquent preacher and then the Jeffreys brothers (Evangelists) had all come from that district. Even before the full Revival they had begun to show their total dedication to the glory of God. Some years later a network of Apostolic, Elim fellowships and Assemblies of God was put in these valleys. At a later stage they would buy out the empty church buildings.

Penybryn Mission, Llangeinor

A small independent Mission Hall, holding about 100 people. Added on later, were a kitchen and a lesser hall, where the Sunday school and the young peoples' fellowship met. In the early days they only used Sankeys. From time to time the downstairs room was let as a family room. The people there speak of times of blessing three times up to 1950.

Caerau Mission Hall (Dyffryn Mission) Nantyffyllon Terrace

The Brethren group is often very reticent about past endeavours but we know that they established a converts' mission in Nantyffyllon as early as 19O5. A likeminded group purchased Dyffryn Welsh Independent church in Nantyffyllon (1908) for £200, by handing over the money to Hope Baptist Church and another in Maesteg.

Figure 15: Opening of Caerau Mission

This was a very old chapel, called 'Ty Cwrdd y Graig' (the Sanctuary on the Rock). Instead of using this very old name, they now wanted to call it Caerau Gospel Mission, but its neighbours knew it as Dyffryn Mission which suggests that former owners had some kind of outreach in mind but then sold it to a new group.

Interestingly enough, W.J. Jeffreys, the father of George and Stephen Jeffreys is listed as a trustee of the Caerau Mission. The building was large enough to have rented accommodation downstairs - and that was where the revered John Holland lived. It also had siderooms for the use of the Band of Hope, a Youth Group, a training class. Part of the basement was used as classrooms on Sundays.

Before Mr. Holland took the leadership, some of the supporters were connected with the Jeffreys brothers and many others insisted that the women members should take part in prayer and testimony. Only a few years later there were new rules, such as - one Church Business meeting per year, one system of offerings in a box near the door, one well-defined statement of faith entered in the Church role. There is no sign of exclusiveness.

As in other Gospel Halls, the brightest of the young people moved away from the valley in the thirties to become schoolteachers etc. These young members met at their Saturday Conference a week after Easter in their Hall. A few went to the Bridgend Conference.

Mrs. Elizabeth Mc'Hale, the daughter of Mr. Holland, one of the founders, has sent in some valuable information. She alone seems to recollect that, although there was a minimum of furnishings in this ex-chapel and only one organ, there was one very striking object. People might be too polite to ask why there was very large marble tablet. It was engraved with the words of scripture. 'We preach Christ crucified.' (1 Cor. ch1. v23). They must have wondered, but some knew its secret.

The leader, John Holland, was a loyal servant of Christ, not men, and governments. He loathed all sorts of violence and refused military service so he was detained in prison. (1916-1918). There, God led him to speak to a stonemason who afterwards promised to make something for John's chapel. In due course, this man sent a marble tablet to be installed in the chapel, as an act of thanksgiving to the glory of God.

Under the leadership of Pastor John Holland, until early in 1943, Caerau built up an unenviable reputation for evangelism. Holland trained a band of young men - telling them to "begin at Jerusalem" instead of itching to go abroad at once. For a short time they associated with the Jeffreys missioners but then they withdrew. They held many open-air meetings. Interest in missions was largely confined to South Africa and the London City Mission. One other outreach was through united conferences in conjunction with two other Gospel Halls. They had a great deal to do with veteran Pastor Len Sparkes and Rev. David Evans. Their finest youth worker was the late Haydn Jones.

Pencoed

The Pentecostalists opened their Zion in Penprysg Road in 1931. The pastors were Henry Harris and the Rev. Albert Griffiths. Their Elder was called Albert Morgan and their Evangelist was Gordon Cave. This little cause set up small house-groups in the expectation of more blessing when the Day dawned when Christ would return to His people. The members are now aged, but a few have stayed on to worship and to witness according to the commission, given in the book of 'Malachi.'

Llanharan

The Gospel Hall here shows a variant form of mission - more like a crusade. The founders had seen modernism spread like a fungus over the teaching in Chapels and Halls, and they were resolved to defend the Word of God. Perhaps they had taken note of an attempt by Bridgend Ecumenical Council of Churches to form an alternative form of instruction. They had appointed the Rev. Ernest Smith who presented them with new interpretations of the Second Coming, the New Age and the Kingdom of God. The energies of many were diverted to Social Crusades during the War so that the Spiritual Vision was fading.

There was another group in Llanharan as well as Pencoed, who were keen on Gospel witness. In 1920, a dozen members of Calfaria had pioneered a Tent of Witness. Next, they found two skilled Evangelists, Mr. Bernard and Mr. Mc'Cullough. Next, they bought an Army hut and were given free use of a piece of land at the end of Rose Terrace. Only one year later, they already needed a new Gospel Hall to increase their activities. There never was a Pastor, so it became desirable to appoint trustees, such as Mr. and Mrs. Doble, John Smith, David Jenkins and Gerald Kingdom.

Finally, there are traces of a branch on the back road via Brynna and Heolycyw to Brynmenyn and Blackmill. We are moving in the opposite direction into the Rhondda Valley.

Preparing the Gospel Hall, 1927

Figure 16: Llanharan Mission Hall

11 *Exciting Events in the Rhondda Valley*

There are only three small townships in the Ely valley and these were centred around King Coal. Going north from Llantrisant, one could see a little Mission Hall in Coedely in which my great-grandmothers' seventeen sons and daughters occupied two pews and could also keep four classes well filled. There were children's meetings before the adults began to attend, wearing scarves and shawls and the best footwear they could repair. Much closer to Tonyrefail was a gap in the terrace where 'Uppingham's Mission' stood. Mr. Uppingham was a very stern and reserved young Gospel preacher.

We must now climb out of the Ely valley and then descend into the Rhondda. The first of the apostolic fellowships was already in being, long before the great advance in the twenties. The earliest of all may have been the Pontypridd campaign of 1911, which the tireless Pastor Dan visited much later, in 1919. It was at a meeting in Mountain Ash that he had met Mrs. Jones of Sion Street, who said God has shown her, six years earlier, that the work should grow in Pontypridd where she herself had received the Baptism of the Holy Ghost and spoken 'in tongues.' Meeting after meeting in her little home, three miles from Pontypridd, people crowded in, seeking fresh blessing. This must surely have been a continuation of the post-Revival prayer and struggle meetings which the English visitor, Holyoake, wrote about in his book, 'The Afterglow.' This is his report.

> "We found the schoolroom nearly full. Something more than ordinary was going on for there was fervour in their prayers and a realization of the immediate presence of God. One man asked, "Are we doing a share of the Lord's work? We thank you tonight because thou hast burdened us with souls. We thank Thee that thou hast opened our eyes and shown us the many who are away from Christ. We feel our nothingness. We are nothing but we are assured that Thou art Almighty."

There is no sign now of an old Mission Hall in North Pontypridd but other hints suggest that a work was going on in the Cilfynydd district and in Hillside, Bryngolwg. They had experienced showers of blessing when Evan Roberts visited them at least three years before the coming of the Apostolic leaders. One precious eyewitness account tells of a meeting in Cilfynydd where the colliery had to be closed and everyone was free to be witnesses. Uncle Ben, uncle to the Rev. M. Russell Jones, tells us how he and his friends planned a march of witness from Pontygwaith to Ferndale. Somehow, he found himself marching the opposite way, down the Rhondda instead and went into a chapel for a Praise Service from eleven o'clock till lunchtime.

When Pastor Dan Williams arrived he announced that he had a special message from the Lord to go up into the Rhondda Fawr Valley, where strong men were waiting for a great event - the Name of God being declared in all His Might. He was called to Blaenrhondda, where men were waiting for an outworking of the Holy Spirit. Unfortunately we have little source material about the Rhondda Fach, but it is common knowledge that Mr. Russell Jones, the nephew, was warmly welcomed, twenty years after the Revival, when a little chapel was set up in Wattstown under the care and prayerful nurture of R.B. Jones's new church, Tabernacle.Porth and Trebanog.

Porth may have been the scene of the first group apostolic witness in the Rhondda. We can share the memories of 92 year old Mrs. Rex. She first of all recalled her mother taking her to all the meetings, then held at Mount Pleasant, Porth, where they worshipped in a carpenter's or cobbler's shop in Davies' Street. They sang without instruments, led by the men, Mr. Rex, Mr. Tom Saunders and Mr. John Arch. Occasionally the children were allowed to prophesy. There was great fervour and love. Mrs. Rex had a special cause for joy at that time.

> "My own husband, after discharge from the Army, wandered into Gospel Services on Tonypandy Square and became a convert and a fervent testifier."

Open-air work was usually done on Cymmer Hill, especially after John Dan Williams urged them on. But they also witnessed in Dinas and in the upper square in Tonypandy - always giving out Gospel messages and tracts.

The links with the Lower Rhondda and the Pontypridd Halls were looser. The official histories emphasise a special conference as early as 1909. It was held at the Park Hotel in Cardiff, where representatives from Glamorgan and Gwent attended. Some wanted a 'British Apostolic Church' and others wanted an 'Apostolic Church of Wales.' The team leadership in and around Porth did not desire to enter any kind of association until after the other Tonypandy group did in 1925.

The fully structured Church in Porth was not formed until 1926, when the foundations of the zinc hut, brought over from a Bristol Works, were prepared by the men who were then on strike. The building was dedicated to the glory of God later that year. From the prophets' 'burdened messages,' they decided they should have five offices - apostle, elder, evangelist, prophet and pastor. The elders discussed the main issues with the church meeting. Any mundane matter was kept outside the church and a decision made on what they called the 'Threshold of God.' Church discipline covered a wide range of matters from head-covering at prayer-times to proper forms of Gospel testimony. Their hut stood near the noisy Rhondda river and the writer can recall the mischievous tricks we tried to commit, when weeknight services were being held. Just beyond this was our primitive football ground. We boys, in faith or daring, used a large sewer pipe to shunt across the whirling, frothing river. One presumes that the apostolic saints had some easier means of access.

Sion, Trebanog

This Mission Hall, at the summit of the Trebanog Pass, which connects the Ely valley with Tonypandy, was an example of the 'better type' of tin mission. Its corrugated zinc sheets protected the beautiful wooden ceilings and some wooden wall-panels. A few benches remain from the 1920's with hinged backs to allow for conversion to working tables or dining tables. A lovely six-sided pulpit with a suitable verse inscription will soon be retrieved and restored. This Mission has had and still has a pastoral leader and it still caters for children's needs. From Trebanog, the top road descends a series of sharp corners and steep gradients into the Upper Rhondda

Tonypandy

We must pass on quickly to the populous Tonypandy and Clydach district, made famous by a boxer and by a Methodist peer of the realm - ex-Speaker of the House of Commons. The first coal owners built a town called Tonypandy which was full of the traditional Welsh chapels. It did have the Central Methodist Hall near the town bridge, whose chief purpose was to provide cheap meals for half-starved children and sick adults during the cruel lockouts of the mid-twenties. This Mission Hall had no brief to evangelise and it seems to have been a practical response to a very significant article, published about 1922. Its main thesis was that the spiritual and moral energies of converted youths needed practical outlets, but that a considerable number of untaught, ungifted people also needed a new kind of recreation, distinct from barbarous games and military drills.

Other essays all gave praise to the Christian Endeavour and Christian Youth organisations who had combined moral teaching and spiritual counsel with physical and mental stimulation. Now they asked,

> "What was to be done for unemployed men and for bachelor lodgers? Why on weeknights should well warmed clubs be open but church and chapel doors shut? Chapels must build somewhere for young people to meet for lantern lectures, singing, library, classes and recreation from 6 to 11 p.m. daily."

Not one of the leaders, Pastor Dan, the Jeffreys brothers, Cynog, Nantlais Williams or R. B. Jones had seen a way to combine holiness teaching with such programmes. The Methodist minister Rev. Gwyther was the ideal man for such a programme. He was practical, sports-loving, compassionate and fully persuaded that God would bless this Mission. The Central Methodist Hall in Tonypandy did its best, as we young people had cause to remember on cold winter evenings right up to the end of the Second World War. Men who dreamed dreams built it. Sadly, one must admit that the recreation and entertainment aspect slowly took over.

There was a similar effort at the original Bush Mission in Clydach Vale, Tonypandy, which had its own leisure centre for unemployed youths. That old Hall has long since been replaced and recently given a bright new stone wall and the appearance of a church. The social rooms seem to have gone. There is a pastor and a counselling room instead. One still marvels at the austerity of these older halls that have no special equipment and no ornamentation. One very reserved informant explained. "We only have our values such as truth, sincerity, and honour."

The Lamb Mission

Thanks to the energy and organising ability of Mrs. W.S. Jones, the minister's wife, the Jerusalem Chapel was able to set up a Mission Hall next to a hotel called the Lamb, which was then badly run down. It was the place where a School for Ragged Children had operated long ago. By good fortune, the writer took down detailed notes of what Mrs. W.S.Jones told him thirty-five years ago.

> "In Ystrad Rhondda, just beyond the Star Hotel, there was a cocoon of dingy lodging houses frequented by navvies and other migrant labourers. One of these had once been a public house called the Lamb Inn. This had hosted a skittle alley and a few private rooms. After this the Inn became a lodging house and the skittle alley was loaned to various organizations such as the Scouts. At one time it was even leased to an undertaker. It was in this private room, attached to the lodging house, that we first held services. The chief helpers were the converts from Jerusalem Chapel."
>
> "How did the Lamb Mission evolve? It was when, in 1910, the Council supplied free meals to the poor children on weekdays while the business community supplied meals on weekends. Local teachers were asked to serve these meals.
>
> "I was then a member of Nebo but I went to the Mission on Sundays and saw a crowd of children hanging about the schoolyard. When I asked if they had ever been to a Sunday school they said they would not come because of their clothes. So I asked the caretaker (the mother of Tom Jones, Club Row) if she could borrow a room.
>
> "The caretaker sent out the wildest boy with orders to bring in as many children as possible. When I returned at 6 p.m. there was a strange silence - but inside the room was packed with children

who were all as quiet as lambs. That same week I tackled the owner of the Lamb Lodging House and asked for one of the private anterooms. This again became packed with children who were now taught choruses and were given a short address as they sat on the floor.

"The next week we moved to a larger room that was once used by the scouts. The planks they had left behind were nailed together to make rough seats which proved to be rather collapsible at awkward moments. Later on we borrowed chairs from Blind Dan's lodging house. We employed the undertaker to make benches and to add on backs to them"

Out of this band of children came many fine converts such as Gilbert Marshman, a Railway Mission worker, and Tom Drummond.

"Why was I doing all this? Because, in a ten-day mission in Jerusalem, I had been so deeply moved."

There were other Independent Missions, some of whom believed they were possessors of the spirit of the Welsh Revival. They all seemed unaware of what other active groups were doing. The Salvation Army had been born in an earlier revival, yet they had nothing to do with the new Mission Halls. Each Gospel Hall was not only autonomous, but also almost unaware of what the next group of brethren was doing. Some groups have felt it wise not to go into detail and the one meeting in Gilmour Street, Tonypandy has been passed by.

Contrast now the way in which the main Apostolic Church strengthened itself, especially after the swift development of other major Pentecostal movements. It was by a subtle process whose aim was unitive and at the same time God-honouring. They would invite independent Apostolic groups to come along to their conferences and hear the pure Word of God. This would be followed by invitations to the kind of group worship that they all loved. Many of these people had felt isolated and unable to do much for the Lord. Now, in those crisis years of social unrest, cynicism and deep discouragement they formed a little group who stood on firmer ground with those others who adopted the 'Apostolic Fundamentals of Faith.' They accepted the same strict code of conduct and their undertaking to pay tithes. Then they were given the same pattern of Ministries such as the teachers and evangelists. This preparation is illustrated in detail in 'Echoes of Grace.'

> "This was our first entrance. The meetings were held in Bethlehem chapel but the place became too small and our Pentecostal brethren then let us use their larger premises. We had a most glorious time - a real sense of coming together of the saints with Israel and Judah made one. They came over heart and soul to the Apostolic order. Some accepted our principles and we then appointed certain men set apart into different offices.
>
> "We feel great joy because the prayer of the Lord that we might be one was fulfilled. Saints everywhere recognize that the cry of the Holy Ghost today is for oneness, for the voice of man scatters but the Lord's voice brings together. Woe to the man who wilfully causes division among the saints and the brethren by false witness. Let us be shut up together and sealed together so that those in the world will say, 'They are joined together and cannot be put asunder.'"

In the next conference, a new pastor was appointed and in due course a prophet was also chosen and provided. Strict examination was made of the doctrines of any group who wished to join them. Then the next annual conference usually gave them the right-hand of Fellowship and, finally, they broke bread together and gave themselves to a time of Praise.

In the case of Tonypandy the Penygroes headquarters wisely found a Rhondda man to be their Prophet. His name was Tom Rees and he must have been intended to be an Apostolic successor to David Llewellyn of Tonypandy. A press release of that period showed how this self-taught miner and theology student had presided over a Spirit-filled assembly when men and women were present, eager for a new vision. "Then the Lord chose from among them His pastors and Elders. Apostles soon came to the fore who planned a wider ministry." David Llewellyn evangelised from Pontypridd to Treorchy and the blessing also spread to the Lesser Rhondda valley - with Porth and Cymmer included.

While the Pontypridd group was conducting local campaigns, the senior leaders in Clydach/Tonypandy held its first convention since the proposed merger in 1922. One speaker pointed to the symbolic meaning of the chapel, which was called 'Trinity', a name that commemorates the 'Eternal Unity.'

> "We also saw its significance as pointing to one fellowship, coming together as the true work of the Spirit since the Spirit unites us whereas carnal man divides us. Since that conference we have a much strengthened movement." (Echoes of Grace. 1922).

Encouraged by Pastor Dan, they held more local Conferences, at Coedpenmaen and Porth and Clydach, which expounded their vision, their beliefs, their gifts, their fruits, and their eternal destiny. The final piece of their strategy was to hold very large meetings in parks and squares, addressed by 'hot-gospellers.' Quiet little groups, like the one at Porth, found themselves out on the streets, witnessing, facing crude hostilities, but reaping souls during those awful years of depression.

At the climax of one such event - the three pastors - Rees, Tonypandy, Saunders of Porth; D. P. Williams, Pontypridd, were inspired to have a united procession through the eight miles of the Rhondda Fawr. Then they turned their attention to the Rhondda Fach, again to Trehafod and above all to Trebanog. Another group visited Ynysybwl and Abercynon once more. These people were the heirs of the revival days and many had gravitated late towards full Pentecostalism- probably in the twenties.

Church planted Missions - An Alternative Solution

During the early twentieth century with the fierce onrush of 'Modernism,' a 'higher criticism' was threatening and certain evangelical churches desired to set up Missions which would both prove the claims of the Gospel and safeguard the Word of God. Prominent among these was Tabernacle Porth, which created and established Penuel, Bethel and Bethlehem.

The modern theories of church planting were not in Tabernacle deacons' minds as they deliberated on setting up actively evangelistic centres for advancing into the future without losing any of their foundational doctrines. Bethel, Penuel and Bethany dealt with all sorts of problems. It was the fourth one - Bethlehem - that came existed purely for evangelism and thorough bible-training.

Even the songs sung in the Infant Department were not about

flowers and bees and fruitful trees. They were frankly evangelistic, for example 'One Door and Only One' or the one called 'God has blotted them out.' The writer's favourite hymn at a very tender age was 'I've found a friend, Oh! such a friend.' The Junior department learned many Golden Texts with a Salvationist theme. All led up to Decision Sunday conducted by an evangelist. After this came the memorisation of three catechisms by all the people and children.

The chapel's only adornment was a scroll saying –'Sir! We would see Jesus,' and a picture in the prayer room was of Jesus praying for those who were about to forsake and reject Him. They believed in a simplified presentation of the Gospel truths, which was very necessary in the raw new housing estate called Mount Pleasant. Even the Anniversary and Demonstration which took place annually had a message for the outsiders, for example the last recital in R. B. Jones' 'The Tabernacle in the Wilderness.' When the great veil was torn away, "At last the way to God's presence had been opened. Now any sinner who believes in the Blood of the Cross, can enter in with boldness and find there a reconciled God."

Week by week, preachers were invited because they were gifted with evangelistic passion and boldness. They included working men born again during the Revival. They included Bible College students also. The Gospel was preached by a long line of prayerful soul-seekers, including a few outstanding women such as Arianwen Jones, Bronwen Hale ,and Sister Sutherland.

How was this Mission governed for forty years? First of all a pioneering group of students managed things then a fulltime evangelist using a demountable hut. About 1925, it was decided to have a Mission Hall and the foundations were laid by miners on strike in 1926, with my own father acting as waggoner.

Meanwhile a membership roll had been formed out of people seconded from the parent church, and placed under four deacons:- later to become six. The Mission also acquired two trained lady workers from Glasgow. Many years later they had a pastor sent out from the Bible Institute.

There is a picture of senior deacon Anthony Dew, digging the first rubble out of the hillside, with other visitors, laying foundation stones for the building. The design seems strange to us because it was a copy of a Riga chapel with a high-pitched double roof. The other noticeable things were the dedicatory texts on the frontal stones. One of these said, 'Christ our only Priest.' The next said 'Christ our only altar.' The third said 'Christ -our only Confessional.' Lastly from a sister church at Trehafod came 'The Word of God-our only Foundation.' So the chief aim of every department had to be a safeguard of the Inspired, Infallible Word and the doctrines therein.

A small group of deacons has run this Mission Hall, who did not make a serious attempt at independence from Tabernacle nor to change into a church, until after 1950. It also kept clear of Association affairs. It had a very extrovert Pastor Watson for several years, then a student pastor nominated by R.B. Jones. Then there was a college tutor who was famed for open-air evangelism. After him came another man who was a remarkable thinker. Slowly the Mission vision faded and the energies evaporated and numbers slowly dropped. But this is the story of many a Gospel Mission after the last war.

Like the Brethren, these chapel sponsored Mission Halls had very little to do with each other. One does not hear of shared campaigns. Separation from the Pentecostal and Apostolic fellowships was even more drastic. By 1927 it was clear that the wise warnings of Nantlais Williams and Mrs. Jessie Penn Lewis, inter alia, were not being heeded.

> "One of the sad effects of backsliding is to make us narrow. Once we lose the love of Christ, it is not long before we show signs of narrowness, in judgment, in doctrine and in conduct. The result is that we are constantly living on the other side of the fence with everyone unable to lift a foot over any stile and unable even to look over the fence at our brethren in Jesus Christ. We have raised high walls between us and the world and we have no desire to go outside with the Word of the Gospel."

Mrs. Penn Lewis made one last warning before her homecall;

> "Let Satan, the separator, be expelled from the saints. Let us stand and fill the gap in the fence by our intercession until Satan is defeated in His aim to disunite, and the Church advances once more towards her goal."

Figure 17: Laying the Foundations of Bethlehem, Porth

12 *Struggles and Battles in the Cynon Valley*

From its beginnings 1907-1910, this movement was clearly divided into the Charismatic or Pentecostalist wing and the smaller group, which stayed largely independent and very Biblicist. They were direct heirs of the Revival outreaches, channelled through three Aberdare ministers. It is easy to overlook the fact that at least four of the Welsh-language chapels kept the flame of Revival smouldering for up to ten years. We owe this knowledge to Parcwyson, the local historian, who attended the prayer meetings at certain churches, which were often presided over by outstanding Revival converts.

> "Thank you for the Breeze, Lord," prayed Tom Howells, "I had thought that you were not going to breathe on our meeting tonight, but the Breeze has come! Grant that we may keep it for we will not do much here without you. Thank you for the arrival of the Breeze, Lord, the Breeze from Calvary's Hill."

Howells' and other converts' consistent testimony was "saved by grace; kept by grace; filled with grace." They were well known figures in The Christian Workers' Movement, organised in 1906. The Mission, described by the Rev. Grawys Jones when Mr. Holyoake visited him in 1908, had begun in 1905, as a Sunday school for ragged and often mischievous children. They found that the parents got very interested. Whereas Cynog Williams of Heolyfelin's group were highly activist and seeking to spread abroad the Gospel, this other team of dedicated young people came along from nearby chapels to teach and guide and to help banish ignorance and immorality. A lady gave £100 to build an iron mission room. This first evangelistic work stayed under the control of Rev. Grawys Jones who insisted that converts should join a church. The room was also used for one weeknight Gospel service and a women's prayer meeting.

At some later stage these workers would have left the parent church after they had formed separate groups. One met on Friday nights for worship in Bell Street, close by an Independent Church, which, for some reason or other, never acquired a Sunday School room. This old church had stone walls, a proper pulpit, a Communion Table, pews and a harmonium, even in 1907. The main supporting family was and are the Beynon family. The other group met at Pentwyn Bach Mission, in Trecynon, which was then under the guidance of a retired Salvation Army officer, Kate Shepherd. They also had house meetings in the homes of Brothers Leach and Forward.

These teams of witness were not all gifted communicators. Some delighted in using their muscular strength to dig trenches and lay foundations for the iron halls, which served their needs. One of these was Abercwmboi and the other was called the Robertstown Mission Hall, which was not erected for the members until 1920, after the troubles. Both of these benefited from the new housing estates. Pentwyn band joined in a project to alter a large house. Then, plans were made to have a Hall, which veterans called Bryn Golwg.

The story of Pabell – the battle of the basements

The Apostolic Movement in Aberdare was founded in 1910 after Pastor Dan Williams had given a message intended for an earnest young man called James Forward. For 5 years, he had been looking for something more and he had been attending all the Conferences. In 1911 at the Pentwyn Mission in Trecynon, the Overseer, prophesied, saying, "Come you on forward!" James Forward was convinced that the Lord had chosen and was calling him. But the young man was still deeply troubled about his future.

Meanwhile, the fellowship had moved to Mr. Leach's house and Pastor Dan and others came to give messages. There were healings and wonderful events.

> “Souls were saved, bodies healed, and the Lord manifested His power and majesty in many ways, with the result that the assembly grew to the number of 60 souls. Praise the Lord!”

But there was also bitter enmity in Aberdare and a great deal of opposition after they had moved to a cellar under the Golden Lion. Their arrival did not come about under the conditions of peace and goodwill. It was far from that.

"The Golden Lion public-house adjoined the house in which the meetings were held, and every time, while the meetings were going on, the landlord of the public-house, under the influence of the Arch-Enemy, engaged men to beat on empty casks and tins. The awful din that resulted was easily heard in the meeting room, the partition between the two houses being of only one-brick thickness. In addition to this a gramophone was placed by an open cellar window, which was right alongside the room where the saints met. This was played the whole of the time the meeting was proceeding. (A matter for much rejoicing and wonder is that the man who usually operated the gramophone is now one of the pillars of the Church, and an Overseer of an assembly).

"In spite of the resultant noise thus created, the meetings went on and the greater the noise of the opposition, the greater the rejoicing and glorifying in the house of prayer. The condition of affairs soon got noised abroad, and people from all parts gathered together to see and hear. Some were sympathetic, some came to ridicule and others came out of sheer curiosity.

"The climax to all this came on one particular evening. The room in which the meetings were held is approached through a narrow lane leading to a passageway. Just over the door of the house is a gangway leading from the upper floor of the public house into the garden at the rear, forming a bridge over the passage. On this evening, the licensee and his wife were in a particularly aggressive mood, being under the influence of drink, waiting for an opportunity to show their displeasure in a practical way. Special preparations had been made to give the saints a good reception. Seven buckets of water had been filled in readiness by the time the meeting ended, and were placed on the bridge overhead.

"But the Lord also had made His preparations. The word came to the Overseer to be keen to His movements and that God would present an opportunity to His servant of which he should be quick to avail himself. The meeting proceeded with the usual mixture of tumult and glory, commotion and threat. As the people were dispersing, the landlady, deceived into believing that the saints were leaving the room below, with a "Now, then! Glory to God!" discharged the contents of a bucket of water on to those underneath. Unfortunately for them and for her, she had made a great mistake, having poured the water onto her own neighbours and customers. One poor woman, who was nursing a young babe, received the full force of the downpour, with the result that she immediately collapsed from shock. In this, the Overseer saw the opportunity of which the Lord had spoken.

"The crowd, becoming incensed by what had occurred, immediately set about having their revenge; a brick was thrown at the gramophone, which caught the horn and put an end to its usefulness. The overseer, with some difficulty, worked his way into the house where the stricken woman was lying unconscious and not responding to any of the attempts her neighbours were making to restore her. Brother Forward, prayed over her, took hold of her hand, and commanded her in the name of the Lord to arise. This she immediately did, to the astonishment of those around, who remarked on the coolness with which everything had been done.

"An hour or two later, what a scene it was at the Golden Lion. A huge crowd had gathered, and, with bricks and stones, wrought indescribable havoc and destruction. Windows were smashed, bottles of spirits and other drinks which stood on the shelves were broken. When the crowd had dispersed to their homes, about two o'clock in the morning, they left the place a total wreck. From that source at any rate there was no further opposition."

God poured out his blessing until, five years later, their new place (Park School) was too small. They had enough resources to build, in Robertstown, a much larger 'Pabell' or 'Tabernacle' (June 1921). Even then, new branches were needed at Cwmbach and Aberaman, where William Morgan, later, became Overseer and then Danny Davies. Other teams moved southwards to Penrhiwceiber, and northwards to Hirwaun.

"The passing years have brought their trials and hardships, joys and sorrows, pains and tears, but, through it all, the patience, guidance and strength of God has been ever present. If the presence of the church in Aberdare can in some ways be attributed to the hard work and faith of the saints, let us not forget that all glory and praise must be due to Him who made it possible and in Whose honour the building stands."

During the last stages of building Pabell, the women and children did the fetching and carrying and fitting, singing praise choruses as they did so. Mrs. Eira Richards testified that there was perfect harmony then. Lighting was by oil-lamps and a large paraffin lamp hung above the pulpit. There was not much heat but they did have a primitive toilet, as well as a boiler house and outhouse. On the Opening Day there was a procession led by three men deacons and three women deacons - Mrs. Baker, Mrs. Lambert and Mrs. Leach as well as the pastor's wife.

"From the first night we had conversions among the young children and young people but there was still much opposition to the movement because of its noisiness."

The chief event remembered by the folk there was the visit of Cornishman, Billy Bray, who preached and praised so fearlessly that people came running in from the fields to fall at his feet. Another famous visitor was Pastor Dan Williams.

Mr. Windsor Jones said, "I went with the young people, witnessing, but we were not baptized by water nor by the Spirit at once. After all, the Lord works in His own ways." Pabell, Trecynon, has it own record of trials and triumphs, tears of joy and sighs of bitterest grief. Yet it is well and strong today under its new minister.

Penywaun

The alternative movement was run on Brethren lines in a district called Penywaun. It was not only an outreach work but also one that practised the highest forms of discipleship. It may have originated from the Welsh side. This lesser known cause has an interesting beginning in that the enthusiasts ventured to buy a disused guesthouse. It was being forced to move into other accommodation, possibly of the iron hut style, but seems to have been very 'go ahead.' Stories were told about their work and it is noticeable that they produced several missionaries. On their honours list were Davy and Gwen Walters of Hirwaun who served in India, Mr. and Mrs. Leonard Gittins of the Belgian Congo and Elved and Phyllis Leigh, who went to Africa. Mr. George Davies of Hirwaun acknowledged that it was zealous workers from the Abercwmboi missions who went over to Hirwaun to commence work there. In one of their campaigns, 97 conversions were recorded.

Hirwaun apostolic church

Hirwaun was at the end of the Revival trail. Hundreds of people travelled there at the height of the Revival period and Evan Roberts warned them severely that they must not be hearers and spectators only but 'doers.' There were thirteen chapels in the township but not one of them provided teaching for the converts and the post-revival story was one of drifting and falling. Blessing returned in the twenties when the teams of witness arrived from Abercwmboi and Trecynon.

The main cause was not established until 1930, when a corrugated iron hut was erected. But long before that, the believers were meeting in premises which had once been a butchers' shop and yard, then a boxing booth, then a fish and chip shop - a strange pedigree indeed! The leader was Lewis Thomas who came over from Cwmbach. There is no known link between the pioneers here and the last survivors of the Revival of 1904. The same is true of at least three other Missions in this area. One possible reason for this is the language barrier, since a large percentage of the 1905 converts came from the Welsh chapels (Bryn Seion, Ebenezer etc.) and went back to their chapels to be faithful witnesses.

George Davies could recall many features of this Pentecostal fellowship at Hirwaun. The building could hold only fifty people at most and it was necessary to have three sessions for Sunday School. The members improvised their own pulpit and communion table. Almost from the start the Redemption Songs had been used for worship and one of the leaders was skilled with the piano accordion and banjo as well. In the summer times they took the young people out into the Brecon Beacons area and would sit singing there until a crowd gathered around them and then they would witness. This fellowship retained the original principles such as no recorded membership, no formal offertory list (such as a collection box by the door), and no restriction in women playing key roles, although it was a man who usually led the Bible Study. As for their beliefs, they eventually adopted the Assemblies of God 'fundamental truths,' which included pre-millenialism. Their teaching about tongues was quite moderate but they are still very separatist in outlook.

Cwmdare Free Evangelical Church

This Gospel Hall has been completely independent ever since it developed from a cottage or schoolroom group by buying a complete army barrack room originally from Dering Lines, Brecon. It is in a beautiful position high above the Dare. It is also a strategic position close to the main school.

Figure 18: Cwmdare Mission Hall

In Cwmdare, in 1911, there were three Welsh Chapels but no English ones. Seven male members of other churches felt they should start another cause in the Tin School at the top of Cwmdare road. Local people still remember Lewis Evans, Daniel James, Will John, Bob Griffiths, John Evans, Eric Collier and Benji Jones the organist. Mrs. Mabel Lewis recollected many wonderful services led by Mother Shepherd of Penywaun who also organized cantatas to raise funds for the new building. She remembers that the village was divided on the matter of giving contributions to the fund. We could not afford to pay for speakers, therefore Deacons came from each Chapel to help start the Work.

> "In 1921, we had enough money to build a Tin Mission. Mr. Tyssul Davies supplied most of the first supply of bricks. Others offered free time to help. A Mr. Harrison agreed to give a piece of land and leased it to the Mission Elders. We purchased an ex-army barrack room which was being used by the Council as a workmen's canteen on the Rhigos road. A Mr. Llywelyn of Fairfield, Aberdare, got permission for them to take thousands of bricks from the old kilns, which had to be cleaned and packed and carried in Tyssul Davies's carts. The building was galvanized without and match-boarded within. This, and the building of toilets and vestry, was done with voluntary labour. The hardest tasks in the next ten years were cleaning the floors and stoking the fires. Mrs. Hilda Davies remembers that, if the wind blew in a certain direction, you could not see who was there."

More people moved in from Dyfed and Powys. When the great Evangelists came, such as David Matthews and Miss Beryl Devine, and Ivor Powell, they had to move the sliding partition back. There was also a trained youth-leader, Alexander Saunders and a Singing School. When they had a Harvest Festival they borrowed the school. Other activities were house prayer meetings and Sunday night Services at the lodging house in Abernant Road. Cwmdare Mission has not produced missionaries, but there was a missionary box in the porch of the Church.

The hall was virtually rebuilt in the forties and extended, to include a baptistry. A deacon told me, proudly, that they still used only the Authorized Version in all meetings. They have had good pastors from time to time, but they seem also to have accepted the New Testament idea of seven ruling deacons.

Central Aberdare

Lastly we come to the Beulah Faith Mission which was unique and which caused no offence to the denominational churches. We went to interview Mr. and Mrs. Mitchell and Mrs. Gerald Jarvis, who were connected with this work. Mrs. Jarvis had heard that, even before her time, there was a Bible bookstall in Aberdare market. The house, now used as Beulah Centre, was dedicated to any form of compassionate work and was the gift of Miss Giles. The retired Mother Kate Shepherd, of The Nook, Aberdare, helped to care for teenage girls in trouble. For a while, three aged women were given food and shelter. Later on, a homeless Christian couple was given food and shelter, and, after that, the Mitchell family lodged there in a basement flat.

All these ventures were under the strict control of the owner, Miss. Giles, who would not permit the group to form itself into some new worshipping fellowship or super-church. Gradually she had worked out a set of aims to place in her Deed of Gift.

To promote the true sense of the fellowship of believers in our Lord Jesus Christ as presented in the New Testament, viz. 'All one in Christ.'

To assemble regularly for prayer, conference and bible study, and for testimony and witness.

To endeavour by life and lip to bring others to the saving knowledge of our Lord and Master, Jesus Christ.

To evangelize and edify through the circulation of the Word of God and Christian literature from the book shop, and to provide Christian workers in all spheres with the necessary material.

To provide Christian literature for pastors, teachers and house to house visitors.

Until the next major developments were made, there was room only for thirty people, but later on, it could take sixty. It had a few padded chairs, a pedal organ and three types of hymnbook - Sankeys, Keswick and Redemption. The reason they had no Communion Table was that they went to their own churches on Sundays. Only one or two broke bread together. There was no Band of Hope, no Christian Endeavour, no Sunday School - only a large Bible Study. Mrs. Jarvis couldn't remember when they started up the Sunshine Corner for children, but she remembers it was largely the work of Myrddin Thomas of Brazil. Occasionally they had the treat of the Magic Lantern.

As a matter of principle, they had no annual meetings and no annual report except that the Working Committee had kept its own minutes, while Mrs. Jenkins kept records of the bookstall. Within terms of the Trust, they were able to give generous unregistered gifts to individual missionaries. All things survived the Great Depression, although they were so short of money and even shorter of trained men. After 1940, there were three specific activities, which had priority. Mrs. Jarvis could also recall the setting up of a Saturday Bible School which prospered for some years. But the three mainlines of Christian witness were the Joint Prayer meeting, the expanded bookshop and the annual Conventions.

Mrs. Jarvis and Mrs. Mitchell could remember those exciting joint prayer meetings, when people came from about eight denominations and fellowships. They could hear almost the last of the Revival converts - Mrs. Thomas of Penybryn - loudly praising the Lord. Hallelujah! Occasionally, Miss Giles took part, but the little room with its flight of steps must have been a problem. The faithful group must have prayed faithfully and passionately for the salvation of Aberdare.

The Bookshop was in existence before the Trust was formed in 1927. Some of the Bookshop Trustees were the Rev. Myrddin Thomas, Glyn Davies and Mr. Jarvis who believed in total secrecy about accounts and donations. Mrs. Jenkins built up the Bible bookshop in the cramped space, which Mrs. Jarvis remembered as the doctor's waiting room before it was sold to them. The working party needed ten years to build up enough resources for a major expansion, i.e. knocking out the old kitchen, removing the prayer-room upstairs and turning the entire basement into a shop with its own flight of stairs. The Mitchell family, father, mother and son, have ministered there ever since. Mr. Mitchell, senior, opened it up to Christian literature and Mr. Mitchell, junior, has added tape and video provisions.

The Annual Conventions

Mr. Mitchell explained how these could be directed and supported by trustees whose terms of reference actually did not include that aim. One word in the Deed, 'Conference,' gave them the loophole. In their prime, the two Conventions made full use of friendly chapels such as Carmel and Bryn Seion. Mrs. Jarvis took pains to explain that her own husband took sole responsibility for the convening, but Mr. Mitchell added that the working party gave something towards the costs. Conference and convention addresses were tape-recorded, but there were still no official reports. For some years, posters were sent to local chapels, from which there was some response. Then parties began to come from Swansea, Carmarthen, Llanelli and Neath. Yet it was still known as the Beulah local Convention.

The author cannot resist disclosing at this point that, from 1938 through to the end of the Communist regimes in Eastern Europe, a certain upper room at Beulah was turned into an amateur broadcasting station. Two Christian refugees from Slovakia came to lodge in the Mission. The husband and wife were skilled in languages and transmitted messages of encouragement to the oppressed Christians. The Work has never been acknowledged publicly by the churches or by any government. This was yet one more example of the faith and obedience of the Trustees, who took the fourth aim of the Covenant very seriously.

This then is the strange and wonderful story of the Mission Halls in Aberdare. Each had a different experience of God's provision and of man's opposition. Each developed its own form of witness and each one its own form of government. In this composite picture Beulah stands out as unique. A totally non-denominational Mission not affiliated to any official Movement and yet making a considerable contribution to the spiritual life of the town.

13 *Evangelistic Missions in the Taff and Rhymney Valleys*

Mr. Jack Cudmore, who now lives in 'The Avenue' in Upper Merthyr, was kind enough to prepare details of all the Halls that he had ever heard of. He was able to help establish the founding date and early history of some of these, although he himself had a great attachment to the Rev. J. R. Morgan's church and Mission in Treharris, which stood halfway down the Taff valley. Morgan's 'Forward Movement Hall,' with its plain seating and equally plain singing and Bible teaching, flourished in the twenties whereas the traditional chapels had dwindled. Children's work predominated for two generations but the witness died out in the fifties because of divisions. Students often served them from Porth Bible College, such as John Evans - who visited fellowships who were willing to support them as potential missioners.

Dowlais

Mr. Cudmore could also recall a few other places much blessed during and after the Revival. In Merthyr, the Forward Movement had shown unusual sympathy with Free Mission work - especially the Ivor Street Hall up in Dowlais among the tough foundrymen. The forty or so believers, who met on weeknights in this Mission Hall, were privileged to have direct teaching from the much-loved Rev. R. B. Jones, the great advocate of consecrated living. In course of time the group broke into three, Twynrhodyn, Penyard (Closed 1970) and Radcliffe Hall in Penydarren. But the post-revival Bible teachers often experienced that kind of disappointment. R. B. Jones' son, Geraint, wrote a tribute in Seren Cymru:

"Week by week he would preach at home on Sunday and then

move off on Monday to do apostolic work in some humble mission too poor to pay him more than expenses. He abandoned traditional forms of Welsh preaching for a new expository style stating the great theological terms of Christianity in the simplest possible way. The only means in hand for both purposes was to relate all truth and all doctrine to Biblical teaching. The Infallible Word had to be the touchstone of the faith."

At one time the group of converts used Godden Memorial Hall. It was this group which moved in 1920 to Ivor Street, where they were taught by Rev. Evan Clement Morgan for very many years. Mr. Morgan's daughter would speak very effectively at Sisterhoods, Rallies etc. She was converted in the Penuel Mission, London, which cared for the needs of scores of housemaids, shop assistants and ambitious clerks. Some of these had brought the Revival fire home with them.

Each Mission preserved its own doctrinal basis. They didn't believe in Church meetings, annual sports or offering lists. They were faithful supporters of missionaries, such as Mansel Thomas. After the main group went elsewhere the remnant drew toward the Elim movement, but was still pretty rigid in attitude. They opened their 'Bethel' which had been given the loan of the Old Co-operative Building.

For years and years, each Mission stood in a completely distinct position and witness from others. Mrs. Roberts claimed that the Dowlais Mission kept its sturdy independence and was ruled by its own elders and deacon. This same lively ninety-three year-old lady was able to tell us how the pastoral work began.

"My father, E.C. Morgan, a deacon at Hebron Welsh Baptist Chapel, had to be deputed to act first as deacon and elder and then as assistant 'pastor' of the new work. The godly Hebron minister gave young Clement all the help he could to study Bible doctrines in detail. After an accident with a horse-drawn tram underground, he had more time to do this work among the Revival converts. In his humble way he did this kind of work for many years. Eventually the Dowlais Mission group felt they should move to the Godden Memorial Hall. E.C. Morgan became an eloquent and dynamic guest preacher at other centres."

As the well-organised Elim Movement gathered force, they ran a

Stephen Jeffreys' Mission in a borrowed Co-operative Movement hall. Several years later, the Elim Trust took control over the Mission and moved its main meeting to a disused school. Once again, the entire work was independent and tightly run by its own body of elders and deacons who urged their young people to alter their mode of life. The witness has not ceased.

Meanwhile the Assemblies of God had developed branches at Bedlinog (E. Griffiths in 1924) and Penrhiwceiber where the Revival had brought much blessing, a generation earlier. Some of these Missions have survived but one informant thought that there was not much spiritual vitality because their first leaders were so unresponsive to the wind of Revival. J. R. Morgan himself preached only once in Merthyr. The larger Welsh-speaking community could always go to Hebron, Dowlais, for spiritual worship alongside the last living revival converts.

Unlike the Aberdare valley there seems to be very little Mission Hall activity down the Taff valley towards Abercynon. The one glowing exception would be Bryngolwg up on the hill. Neither does one find much sign of new life on the high moorland between the Taff and the Rhymney rivers. The nearest was Fochriw, in its own shut-away valley in the shadow of the pits. Despite its unlikely environment, the believers have long since built a Mission Hall and remained active Christians. We hear also about a small Mission called Deri situated in yet another narrow ravine on the border of Glamorganshire. Somewhere, closer to Bargoed, was a very private apostolic mission group, who exercised strict discipline in the interests of spiritual growth and moral purity. No details about their mode of worship have been divulged, but it was definitely not a Mission. Theologically they were sound, but they were taught that no group activity had any validity if the holder of any one of the five offices were not present, the apostle, the prophet, the evangelist, the teacher and the elder.

Some Mission Halls were encouraged by older chapels of an evangelical kind. In the case of Saron, New Tredegar, the enthusiasts had gathered every night waiting for the fire of the Spirit to descend. They must have moved on to nearby Deri or to smaller mission fellowships, such as Fochriw, where the women and girls too, prayed freely along with the menfolk and where the shyest attender was encouraged to take part.

Cwmsyfiog

This Mission already had a small fellowship which had branched off from the Bargoed area, where believers had already created a new church called Caersalem, Aberbargoed, and who had decided, prayerfully, to erect a plain school chapel for classes, prayer meetings and three Sunday morning services per month. A proper chapel, Bethel, was built and opened in 1898, according to our Baptist archivist, William Jones. The older school chapel was given over to a temperance movement, known as Rechabite Tents. About seventy English-speaking Christians worshipped at Bethel, while an ex-farm boy, John Francis of Brithdir, served their pastoral needs. But the fruitful time was yet to come because the Rev. Morgan Lewis of Coedpoeth became their evangelist-pastor in 1901 and vastly increased the numbers and influence of this mission during and after the Revival years.

Figure 19: Gospel Church at Cwmsyfiog

Cwmsyfiog had become separated from its mother church and set up its own system of gift recording, enrolling and conduct of meetings. The Church kept its Welsh-English hymnbook and Welsh-English Bible and had a normal Membership Roll, a Statement of Faith and a proper record of gifts and contributions. It seems that this Mission gave no roles to women, except to teach children and women's classes. It was a Mission Hall in the sense that it fostered a very large Sunday school, yet it did not believe in uniformed organisations for youngsters.

When Albert Turner became pastor, there was a new interest in open-air witness. There was a Christian literature work and there was wide-spreading interest in missionary work overseas, but no one can remember anyone actually going overseas from this Mission. Albert Turner and his family lived by faith without any stipend at first, but 30 shillings a week was given later. His leadership of this Mission followed that of Rev. Morgan Lewis, who also had no salary from the church. Recently, someone has renovated and redecorated the chapel. They have inserted some striking panels and scrolls on the outside walls. Perhaps this reflected the lively nature of this congregation or was it the idea of the large youth group whom Albert Turner led? Perhaps it was his vision and energy.

Tabernacle, Hengoed

This also started as an unacknowledged branch when Mr. A.L. Morgan and his people had withdrawn from the Baptist chapel, Mount Pleasant at nearby Maesycymmer because of the rejection of the Revival converts by deacons who had no truck with revivals nor Keswickism. The group met at first in the Coach House belonging to Brooklands House in Maesycymmer, which was the home of a Cardiff businessman, A. L. Morgan. Eventually they built a stone chapel of their own on wasteland near the railway arches.

No radical change took place in Tabernacle's hymnody and confession of Faith and they held regular church meetings, after it built its sanctuary. Those were happy days, when the Rev. Roy Lane Morgan was ordained for service with the B.M.S. in North India, and Rev. D.J. Davies for pastoral work. Those were very memorable days, when Mrs. Jessie Penn Lewis came to speak, or when the charismatic David Matthews (evangelist) conducted a short mission. Unfortunately there were hidden currents in Tabernacle. This came to a head in a dispute about the sustentation fund because a new group was splitting away to form the Gospel Hall in Ystradmynach. The members said they couldn't support the work on a revised annual grant. Rev. Morgan Lewis then decided to accept a call to a new venture at Cefn Hengoed.

Bethel Mission Hall, Cefn Hengoed (Formed 1921)

According to the Efengylydd magazine, which published monthly reports about the Home Mission of Wales, Mr. Griffith Hughes arrived at Garden City in Hengoed in 1919 and was replaced by Mr. Matthew Francis, another evangelist. He was described as a man of ideal make-up, on fire with zeal to win souls for the Son of God. His whole desire was to be burnt out in His service. The hospitable people of Hengoed showed great concern for Matthew and his boys. As always, this drew in children first, but afterwards the parents came in rather nervously and enjoyed the informality. Local people provided cottages for prayer and house-meetings until 1921. In the twenties, coal miners on strike laid foundations and volunteers came forth to raise the walls of Bethel. Principal Edwards dedicated it in 1921, with Rev. W.S. Jones as guest preacher.

Unfortunately Matthew Francis felt frustrated because his portable hall could not be used for the children's work and was so dilapidated that it was replaced by a large tent. In Matthew Francis's last half year, a whole lot of children and young people came to the Lord.

The Rev. Morgan Lewis came from Tabernacle and took charge, a man of prayer as well as of a man of song. His wife, daughter and three sons were equally musical. During his pastorate, the Mission hall was reconstructed in 1933 and rededicated. At the same time the Mission ceased and a Church was formed with a proper constitution where all the enrolled members could take part, as long as they agreed with the Statement of Faith.

It took many a year of sacrificial giving to engage in building a proper Hall with about one hundred and fifty seats. It was always a very conservative place with bare swing-back benches and a very plain pulpit. Alexander's' hymns and Sankeys' 'Songs and Solos' were the staple diet, but a special book of CSSM choruses was used with the children. Only the A.V. King James Bible could be used and only men conducted the Bible studies and weeknight prayer meetings. There was no uniformed organisation but the Church encouraged support of Christian Literature Ministries. There was a stronger commitment to Christian Endeavour and also to missionary work. It was their privilege to send off Miss Dilys Morgan to do faithful service with the Ceylon and India General Mission.

Up to and through the years of World War II, Rev. Morgan Lewis had the full help of his son, Emlyn, who also had a lay-preaching ministry in the valleys, prior to his Bethel pastorate. The writer makes no excuse for telling the story about Emlyn. Like his father, he would usher any guest speaker to the rostrum and then say in a loud whisper. "Do you wish to warm up the meeting or shall I?" If you said, "Please do!" you became the object of a passionate prayer, which charged the atmosphere with Power.

Both father and son adopted a paternal ministry, with people coming to them for advice and not direction. Two generations would get married there, bring their children to Sunday school, dedicate some and pray for conversion for others. Those generations would work for the Lord until they were finally committed to Heaven. Their pastors' prayers and presence were always with them.

Calvary Baptist Mission, Penybryn, near Gelligaer

This was founded in 1926, near the end of the growth period. It was not a breakaway cause, but a deliberate 'church plant,' organised from Cefn Hengoed. It had very plain furniture, swing back chairs and no pictures or plaques. Its songs were from Alexander's, Sankeys and Golden Bells. A great number of children turned up regularly because of the new housing estates in Penybryn. During the General Strike of 1926 many fathers lent a hand to do the foundation walls.

A congregational type of policy-making body ran the church from January 1931 onwards. Apart from the witness on the estates, there was a lasting interest in missionary work overseas. The only full time trained officer had been trained at Matlock Bible College. Two other men were very well known lay-preachers.

English Baptist Mission, Ystradmynach

Our only informant is senior trustee, Mr Webb, who was a little lad when the Mission was built during the first war. Mr Williams, director of London House Millinery in High Street, opened it, free of debt, in September 1916. He and his business friends became trustees and deacons. Some of them had left Maesycymmer chapel because they were far more zealous than the average member. They took instant steps to collect funds and then put up a brick building, which took the place of their corrugated zinc hut, named 'Y Clawdd,' which stood on Commercial Street between the Royal Oak and the Workman's Hall.

In the new Hall, there was seating for sixty people on long benches with reversible backrests made out of pitch pine. There were dedicated hymn boards and a communion table. A movable pulpit covered the baptistry. The only ornaments in the Hall were beautiful pewter cups and plates. There was a Glow Worm coal fire stove with a flu pipe going out through a side wall.

This Mission has held its own deeds, kept in a Blackwood solicitor's office and has it own independent Statement of Faith. Church meetings were quarterly and women took an equal part. All members had to be baptised believers.

Preaching was entrusted to ex-students from the Barry Bible Institute (originally at Porth.) On special days, such as Whitsun and the Church Anniversary, they could get R.B. Jones himself to preach. From 1920-1939, there was a pastor named Shuttleworth and after him the Rev. Kenneth Peel. There was also a colporteur, working from the market. The senior deacon was Everson the grocer and Mr. Meads was the superintendent.

There were two offerings, one on the Lord's Day and one at the weeknight meeting. There was a very informal method of collecting funds for the work and there were also 'Gift days.' The building was enlarged in 1940 and much improved two years later.

Llanbradach

This Mission was always Baptist in its confession and practice, but would have nothing to do with Association or Union. Its long serving pastor was D.J. Williams who never gave up his secular employment. He went to Porth Bible Institute, as a day student for training, and amazed everyone with his gifts of evangelism. He told the author in a letter that several were saved when hearing one of his 'trial sermons' and the promise was fulfilled in his ministry. The inspired, infallible scriptures were a Rock upon which they stood.

Caerphilly

The name of Caerphilly, Assemblies of God, appears on the official list compiled in 1924. It was situated in Pandy Road in the downtown district called Pontygwyndy. Nowadays it has a pastor but in the beginning it had one Leader who invited those, attending morning meeting and putting their freewill offering into a wooden box on the Lords table, to turn round and face the people and give a word of testimony or a prophecy. It was permissible to use a harmonium and an accordion because they often went out into the open air to witness in other parts of the town. Like the Salvation Army, they liked to use a few tambourines. Women and children could join in the worship and at times an accordion would be used.

No doubt this survey is not the whole story because Mission Halls tend to come and go and get forgotten by men, if not by the Lord 'who is no man's debtor.'

14 *Four Great Missions in the Western Valley of Gwent*

The Sirhowy and the Ebbw valleys, which run side by side, had very different experiences of the Welsh Revival of 1904. Revival preachers came over to the Western Valleys ten times more than to the Eastern Valley.

The chief centres for Revival activity in the Western Valleys were Rogerstone, Newbridge, the Blackwood district and Ebbw Vale with Beaufort. The South Wales Argus reported several hundred conversions, but more than a half of these fell away swiftly, having expressed much conviction of sin but nothing more. Half of the rest formed their own Mission halls and many stayed in their own Churches.

Rogerstone Mission

The first product of the Revival was the Tin Mission, sited very close to Keene and Nettlefolds, who had long since moved their workforce from Shropshire to Monmouthshire. The Mission was born in the age of horses. There were horse-drawn carts, paraffin-oil carts, milk carts and brewery carts. The hearses were horse-drawn, and even the first buses were pulled by horses. It was a time of darkness until 1909, when the first gas lighting was tried out. It was a period dominated by the whistles from the works and the whistles from the railway sidings. In the long hours, during the night, one could hear the shunting engines and their subdued hissing. All through the day the foundry hooters dominated the timetable.

Many of the workingmen were hardly aware of the religious life of their forefathers, until a number of marvellous events altered this and other communities for a generation. In 1905, in the full flush of the Welsh Revival, Bethesda, in Upper Rogerstone, had full prayer meetings, passionate singing and a strong desire to live up to its name – 'House of Mercy.' There were some deacons who had the inspiration to look down the hill to the huddled workmen's houses near the foundries. They realised that, should such men and women be touched by the Revival, they would be totally out of place in the top Chapel, where lawyers, doctors, teachers etc. were wont to meet. It was decided that they should make some sort of a bridge to the 'publicans and sinners' in the Nook.

In 1906, a plot of ground was given to Bethesda Church, rent free, by Mr. Thomas of High Cross, in order to put a Mission Hall on the lower road. Commonly known as the Tin Mission, the hall was one of at least two dozen sturdy buildings in the valleys. Their strong wooden panelled walls were enclosed in corrugated iron sheets. Unfortunately they were intended to be temporary halls, without proper foundations and without any ground drainage. The Tin Mission site at Rogerstone had thirteen steps leading up to it that caused no problems to the vigorous young families of the converted people. There were many conversions; the most significant of which was that of Mark Roden, who preached the Gospel until his 90th year. The parent chapel found volunteers to go down to the Hall to conduct weeknight services and a Sunday night Service. These volunteers included Moses Evans and Fred Lewis. Many people helped develop this work, seeking no reward or status. When Mr. Roden was too old, Miss Nellie Lewis (Mrs. Gregory) took over.

There were two particular periods after the Revival, when there were further significant blessings. One of these was a Mission conducted by a Mr. Russell and his One-to-One Band. The other period was a kind of student ministry, entrusted for a few years after his Bible Training Institute courses, to the Rev. Myrddin Russell Jones who was dynamic! The result of all this was a flourishing cause until the thirties and the Depression when the removal of the works from Rogerstone to Cardiff denuded the Hall of its male workers. Despite this terrible setback, the sisters' work had begun under Miss Nellie Lewis and Mrs. Ifor James and there were plans for a new development when the dark days were over.

Unfortunately another dark shadow was looming on the horizon and that was the condition of the Hall. It was still only forty years old, but the floorboards were rotted and pitted and the ladies, led by Mrs. Friend, had to scrub them. Mrs. Catherine Brown could recall the heating system, called a tortoise stove, a tall iron structure, with a carved tortoise on the top. When one opened its mouth, i.e. the lid, a ferocious heat came out and one had to feed it with coal from a broad shovel.

The Band of Hope and old folk alike, loved to sit close to it and one sparsely clad little boy often went to sleep. Occasionally, the tortoise became nasty and filled the Hall with black smoke. The roof was sound but the windows left much to be desired. It made very hard work for the ladies of the Sisterhood who were young mothers then.

In 1941, there was another blow in the form of a letter from the local authority, commandeering the Hall for the storage of goods belonging to bombed-out families. It was not released again, until 1942. Eddie was a Sunday school lad and he insists that they still used part of the Hall and that there was furniture stored in the back part. Meetings were held in houses during the worst of the blackout months, but wartime difficulties discouraged attendance and the sacraments were observed in the parent chapel. When the Hall was refurbished, Mrs. Gregory was appointed to officiate at Sunday evening services and to reconstitute the Sisterhood. After her day, the cause was served by deacons and then by Mr. Marshall, Rev. B. P. Jones and Mr. Brian Ford. During Rev. B. P. Jones' pastorate in the sixties, the members took another step of faith and self-sacrifice and accepted their removal to the Cefn Wood estate, where they and Bethesda erected a purpose-built Chapel.

A Pentecostal Hall, name unknown, also appeared in a bought 'ex-chapel' building in Rogerstone. It served their needs until they could build a larger place a little way up the old lower road. There does not seem to have been any Gospel hall in neighbouring Risca.

Crosskeys

In about 1910, an evangelist called Valdez held meetings at the Central Hall in Newport and electrified people by publicly setting a lady free from a grotesque goitre. Shortly after this a Mrs. G. in Wattsville was healed of cancer "sitting on an ordinary chair." Perhaps the greater type of miracle was that 'prayer-brothers' were convicted that they had to be cleansed. There was much confession needed by them of hidden sin and harsh words.

A group of Revival converts continued to meet in Mrs. Eatwell's house under the guidance of Josiah Purnell, but the first flush was over and God came down to stir them again. An attempt to set up their own Hall was stifled by the officers of Zion, Wattsville, who opposed the doctrine of the Second Coming.

Later on, a crisis was reached when Mrs. Watts preached in her chapel on the Second Coming in the summer of 1912 and was asked to resign. The small group had been meeting for intercessory prayer and was now invited to make use of her own home in Hafod in Tudor Terrace for worship and Bible-study. A Mr. Tom Mills of Islwyn Road also offered a room for prayer times, but this was not convenient.

Figure 20: Crosskeys Mission Hall - former billiard room

These young people were bitterly attacked by the community as 'Second Comers.' The Hicks' family and the whole family of the Mercy's, were soon joined by very many seekers after truth. Search was made for a roomier place and someone walking out with Tom Hicks noticed the deserted billiard room in Crosskeys. They promised to pay its owner £400 in two years. They cleared that debt by rigorous tithing and by repairing whatever could be saved. The first converts were so quiet and gentle that people forgot to slander them. Yet they fell into disfavour with their churches because of their beliefs in the 'Second Coming of Christ' and in the need for 'full immersion.' After a while they were compelled to leave those parent churches. One day, in August 1914, they all went down to the Lighthouse at the mouth of the Usk where stood a little church with a baptistry. Their faithfulness to the Lord's command was rewarded by experiences such as the midnight prayer meeting on Twyn Barlwm, where they all fell to their knees.

> "The Dear Lord met us in a wonderful way and, 'Heaven came down our souls to greet, and glory crowned the mercy seat.' So near were we to Heaven that we felt we could hear the song of the angels. We came down from the mount that morning filled with joy and the Holy Ghost, enjoying a new experience with our Lord, one we would never forget."

In the years, 1914-1921, they were seeking new truths all the time. Some went all the way to Sunderland to sit under Rev. Alexander Boddy's ministry and eventually receive what Mr. and Mrs. Hicks called "Baptism in the Holy Spirit with the Biblical signs of speaking in tongues." Others went to the Llandrindod Convention in August 1914 to learn all about full consecration. A small party went to the Bangor Convention in Northern Ireland, led by Pastor George Jeffreys. It was then that the future founder and pastor of Golden Grove, Newbridge, Leonard Jenkins, received his personal enduement. The last group fell under the influence of healer-evangelist Howton of Glossop, who was the instrument by which the remarkable 'Dad,' Sidney Mercy, came into personal blessing.

So many were coming now that the Crosskeys leaders stepped out in faith and bought and converted the billiard room which at first looked like a shed. Witnesses say that on the first day of possession they received a message in 'tongues' and were assured of much blessing, which has been fulfilled over and over again. It is quite a thrill to walk into that sanctuary today and see before you the scrolled text 'Holiness unto the Lord' and to recall how many pioneers stood at this pulpit before it was replaced by a lectern built over the baptistry.

Another big event took place about 1923, when the Assemblies of God movement recognised them at last and they gladly signed the 'Fundamental of Fundamentals.' The first four clauses of this document are Bible honouring, Trinitarian, Salvationist and Holy Spirit honouring. Proceeding to Clause 5, we read about Baptism in the Holy Ghost, the initial evidence of which is the speaking with other tongues as the Spirit gives utterance. They also taught deliverance from sickness which was provided for in the Atonement (Isaiah ch.53 v.5). They expected the pre-millennial coming of the Lord Jesus Christ as the 'Blessed Hope before all believers.' The last clause again emphasised the gift of the Holy Spirit and the Offices that have been set by God in the Church. (1Cor. ch1 and Eph. ch 4. vs7-16)

For the next ten years the work grew too rapidly for its building and there was a growing range of outreach activities plus a generous policy in regards to sponsoring individual missionaries overseas. In this busy Hall, there were meetings seven nights a week, plus Saturday afternoon Bible-class. Tom Mercy, who had a roving commission, was so blessed that, by 1934, he was the founder of many little assemblies, such as Cwmfelinfach, Bedwas and Earlswood. The leadership at Crosskeys passed to Wilfred Mercy, a man full of the Joys of the Lord. Ambitious plans were being made for a series of great conventions to be addressed by teachers such as Donald Gee, Wilson, Cove, Burton, Howard Carter etc. Extra benches were placed on the tiered rostrum area below a magnificent organ. One corner of the room was called the 'Hallelujah Corner.'

Fortunately Mrs. Mills recorded her own memories of the old chapel before the new preaching centre was built in 1934. Her memoir showed clearly that the congregation was made up of the humble people of these communities. An eighty-verse ballad, written in 1957, names the families on their pilgrimage - going onwards because of a divine vision. The poet gives their occupation as checkweighmen, firemen, hawkers and drapers, - all well versed in scripture. The poems also refer to missionary sponsorship and to church planting by Tom Mercy, here, in South Wales. Often, after a bout of remarkable healings, there would be a forward surge.

The new hall (March, 1934) was a striking building, erected on allotments. Volunteers once more did the basic work. Yet another

£16,000 had to be found because they wanted classrooms and anterooms and all-through electricity. All furniture from the billiard hall sanctuary was scrapped and new hand made benches and seats installed. In front of this were four tiers of seats that were filled by visitors on Conference days. They had a choice of great Bible teachers. On the official Opening Ceremony there were twenty-four pastors and evangelists present and three leading members of the Mercy family. Incidentally this occasion was used by some visiting speakers to speak glowingly of the general growth of the Pentecostal cause in Wales.

Golden Grove, Newbridge

Leonard Jenkins developed the work at Newbridge, using an old farmhouse, which still stands on the main street. We hear of two gifted women preachers (some called them prophetesses), Mrs. Bell and Mrs. Dixon.

Figure 21: Where Newbridge Pentecostals first met

The members here had to do battle with unemployment and serious shortages. Yet they still gave generously and regularly to the Mission work. At first, they used an old farmhouse alongside the main road. Their first building down in the neglected part of Newbridge was slowly enlarged, as they bought more and more of the disused Zion chapel.

It was very spartan inside with no texts and no pictures and a curious absence of flower vases. The great strength of this cause was its musical witness presenting the Gospel. They were also quite good at open-air witness. Nowadays it is well served by the Palmer family but for fifty years it enjoyed the pastoral work of one man.

Oakdale Baptist Mission

This was a rare early example of 'planting' by a deliberate choice of a Home Mission. The main lines of action had been set out thirty years before by Dr. William Edwards the Principal elect of Cardiff Baptist College. He argued that a Mission Hall would need an evangelist, a colporteur, a supervisor at least to visiting 'sisters of the people' and an agreement that local Baptist ministers should give occasional ministry.

As the 'Rhiw Sir Dafydd' estate expanded, just before the Great War, a Mr. David Hussey was set up as a paid evangelist and workers came over from three chapels. They were no longer content with the Moses Watkins Hall, so they moved their contact meetings to the local school. This was a temporary move while they were forming a proper Church, in 1915 and while they were converting a former barn, by voluntary labour.

The new building was called a schoolroom but it swiftly matured into a recognised Church, managing its own affairs. Eighty years later, in a much improved Hall they can celebrate how many classes of children have passed through their hands and been led to Christ. The author was thrilled to view a hundred or so slides for their Lantern lectures and they still have the machine. For years they have sung the old Gospel songs and told the same 'old story that is ever new.'

Cefn Fforest, nr. Blackwood

This was another of the Missions planted directly by the Association in the Garden City village estates built by the Powell Duffryn Coal Company.

The idea was to send David Hussey there for two years, but unfortunately, some of the local opponents objected and he was forced to move his people to a large house in Penylan Avenue. Because of such delays, a corrugated iron building was opened, so children, as well as adults could shape the actual services. When Rev. Morgan Lewis agreed to mastermind their Sunday school programme, he walked into a very plain Hall. It had swing-back benches, a dais, a lectern and a place to keep two large very ornate registers one for membership and one for gifts and offerings.

A very calm period followed, from 1916 to 1924, under Mr Addis's leadership. Then this Hall, like the nearby Pentecostal Mission, suffered great loss during the Depression, when dozens of promising young Christians went off to the cities.

Pontllanffraith

This branch Mission has been in existence since the thirties when the Mercy family served them well. Like all the others, it began humbly in 11 rented rooms, but it has grown quite a bit and is a meeting point for Pentecostal families scattered here and there up the Rhymney and Sirhowy valleys.

Waunllwyd, Ebbw Vale

This chapel is a curiosity in that it behaved for a while like a Pentecostal meeting yet it was confined to a few chapel members, two or three deacons, the Pastor T. M. Jeffreys and a group of seven new converts, with twelve more coming up from Cwm. At first, its house groups set up links with the British Pentecostal Conference, not with the Welsh Apostolics associated with Pastor Daniel Williams. They preferred the small house-group system. Madoc Jeffreys observed, after he left, that many of these little groups lacked a teacher and were prone to pick up strange doctrines.

"They need to be taught, for instance, that the wonderful emotions, liberated in the soul by the Spirit of God, must need also be controlled by the same Spirit and not indulged in riotously."

Unfortunately this was forgotten at Waunllwyd Chapel which never proceeded to the Mission Hall stage for better outreach.

Beaufort, Sardis

The chief witness was the apostle Purnell, who was converted when 13 years old, towards the end of the Revival. He worshipped zealously at Zion, Brynmawr, but then lapsed and became lukewarm. After his marriage, he attended Zoar, Beaufort and heard the invitation to give himself entirely to God. A couple of years later, he heard a Voice saying loudly, "Leave this place and go and do My will!" After he obeyed, he began to pray in tongues.

Sometime later, they had talks with Pastor Dan and with Prophet Jones Williams. Then, they were formed into a proper assembly or fellowship. They applied to use the local school on Sundays, from August 1921 onwards. They eventually moved from a 30 seat room to a 300 seat hall.

> "Every night we held cottage meetings. Our homes were the Lord's and every room was occupied with crowds coming. We took this spoiling of our goods joyfully. God was working, saving. Skittlers, boxers and card-sharpers were swept into the Kingdom. Drunkards, and swearers alike were saved. We saw, and still have on record twelve years later, some miraculous cases of healing. God was baptising many in His Spirit, who then began speaking in tongues and prophesying. Without the touch of any human hand, prophetic channels were born in Revival power. We were enabled to erect a stone building, called Bethel in April, 1923. Formal membership rose from 7 to 80 and then doubled. Help came from Pastor J.O.Jones, Pastor Jones Williams and Pastor James from Pontardawe."

Purnell believed that all the new work began with a word of prophesy which led to a word of blessing. One of those prophecies led Purnell down to Newport to begin the work there. Meanwhile, the Beaufort group organised conventions, which drew about 900 people to the town, and the watch-night service drew about 400. Visitors noticed the total unity of officers and members.

"In a while, I met two angels in the persons of Brother Tom and

James Seabourne. True as steel they joined with me in open-air work and, shortly after, another came along, making four in all. We decided to rent a meeting place, the name of which was Sardis."

Tirzah

The entire history of Tirzah is a precursor. It was clearly designed to be a Sunday School Room, plus a children's centre. It was used extensively up to 1919, when a stone Chapel replaced the Hall. For over forty years it did duty for a variety of bodies. They began to baptise their own and Caersalem's own young people, but it was still in a brook not in a Baptistry. Both chapels proved that these public baptisms were a source of speedy growth.

The chief figure of the period was Mr. Harry Howells (1860-1920), 'Wise in counsel, loving in fellowship and utterly loyal". His brother was the first Missionary to go from Tirzah and became the Principal of Serempore Theological College.

This Mission became more and more open-ended towards the end of the century. They had a full executive council, with a librarian. They also had an IBRA Secretary. All of this shows it was intended to be no more than a Mission Hall or School.

Finally, in the I930s, they had Young Life Weeks, Young Worshippers' League and a Young Covenanters Movement. The various Missionary activities continued until the two World Wars severely weakened all this work. The last significant thing the Mission did was to draw up guidelines for the potential leaders of the Sunday school and the young peoples work. A list of ten rules was proposed and seconded and passed, as of general use, by the young people in the Church meeting.

15 *Compassionate Missions in the Eastern Valley*

The after-effects of the Welsh Revival were very limited in this valley and there is no evidence that Pontymoile Mission was touched at all. Three of the four Mission Halls in the Pontypool area have quite different origins. The Abersychan and Blaenavon area had strong Pentecostal associations but we begin with one that was completely independent of the others.

Bethel Hall

The Bethel Hall, High Street, Pontypool was formed from ex-Pontymoile Mission members after the death of Mr. Wintle, their founder. This Hall was a non-sectarian gathering of about twenty very earnest Christians. They met in a single room, with a side annexe, but still managed to cope with children's work. All worship was severely plain, but there was a little harmonium. Mr. Dykes was happy to invite preachers from different persuasions. These earnest and spiritually minded attendees accepted the strict rules governing conduct and relationships and even on the type of music they sang. It was ruled by Mr. Dykes and a few elders and it lasted Mr. Dykes' and his family's lifetime.

Broadway

This was an Apostolic Church, which was set up just below a new housing area called the Wern. Our informant said that it was intended to reach out first to the children and then to the parents, but it gradually lost that vision. Its building has the usual austerity inside, where there were no plaques or pictures but there was a large text-scroll. Unlike some of the early Apostolics, they had a special Communion table, on which a single cup and a single plate were put when required. Apart from the tithing, there was a freewill offering, which the people brought up to the table and placed in a special 'Lord's Box.' Everything was geared to close fellowship with each other in the fold. Outreach work on the nearby Wern estate was limited to one or two open-air meetings. Some of this work was a casualty of the Second World War, when the few available men were doing extra long shifts on the railway and in the foundry. Their only outside contact was with their own conferences in Swansea, Penygroes and Cardiff. Their favourite Gospel singer is still among us, now in her hundredth year.

Assemblies of God, Osborne Road

The story of the AOG Mission in Pontypool is a story of slow preparation, sudden success, equally sudden failure, long slow recovery and a new launching out called Sharon. The 'Penties' were said, at first, to be worshipping in the 'Coop shop.' After a period of sacrificial giving, they built a hall on the other side of the Afon Lwyd bridge. The Hall had a spacious platform and not a pulpit. It also had a side hall. From this new base, the group went out for open-air witness in Osborne Road , George Street and Waunfelin Road. Occasionally, they used a large room above Fowlers' the Draper.

The arrival of Mr. Howell Harris the evangelist changed a whole situation. For a few years, the Hall was filled, two or three nights a week. The leaders took thought to form a branch in Griffithstown. Then arose the old enemies of scandal, division and confusion. The main work collapsed and the Hall became a Salvation Army Hall. The remnant moved eventually to a house called Llwyn Onn in Waunfelin Road and became nothing more than a house fellowship, except that they had a lady-worker called Vera Humphreys. Further progress was held up until they could recover their unity and vision and felt able to support a pastor. This is the group which had the thrill of turning an old garage into the Sharon Mission Hall on Osborne Road.

Pontymoile Mission

This Hall is in the ideal position for a mission rather than a place of worship because the valley roads and the West-East route cross each other at this point. Its story has been told in booklets such as Mr. Collins' 'Pilgrims All.' From 1855 to 1875, the future founder of the Mission never entered a Sunday school or a place of worship, but, in 1875 he married a God-fearing girl from Blaenavon where her father was Master Roller, whose witness and prayers moved upon his heart. Thomas Wintle worked briefly at Siemen's works at Landore, where he was deeply shaken by a fatal accident to a Christian lad who prayed for the salvation of his fellow workmen even as his body was being consumed by fire. Almost at once there was Revival in that area and Thomas Wintle 'arose and came to his Father.'

Figure 22: Pontymoile Mission Hall

He promised to serve God, but not as an evangelist. He plunged into temperance works and founded a good Templar's Lodge and also supported the Blue Ribbon Movement and the Rechabite Movement. Gradually, he realised that many needed to know the Gospel. In June 1878, he began to preach in a cottage. The 'Witness' reached and blessed many adults. It is said that he also preached from a large stone on the roadside opposite the Tavern in Cwmynyscoy. As winter approached, he and his wife found room for another opportunity, in their own house, called Bethany, 'The house of Bread.' He noticed bands of ragged, uneducated and badly starved children and opened a 'Ragged School' in a disused granary.

One year later, they procured an iron building for their expanding work. Ten years later, they erected the Pontymoile Hall, consisting of the Hall, a rescue home for girls, run by Mrs. Richards, the Institute and the Coffee Tavern. In the same ten years, they opened branches in Pontnewydd, Cwmffrwdoer and George Street, Pontypool. Two of the trustees purchased the Dowlais Hall and appointed a resident missioner.

Mr. Wintle visited all these regularly, as well as the County Jail. His health broke down because he was trying to be an activist worker, a manager, an organiser and teacher, as well as working as a draughtsman. He was advised to choose one or two areas, when friends and wife noticed his extreme tiredness, for example- when going to the 3 a.m. shift on a Monday after going to three services on a Sunday. Prayerfully, he chose the unpaid voluntary work, which meant great sacrifices. As they had no children, his wife also became heavily involved. A close friend, Mr. Morgan who owned 'The Christian,' reported that she was becoming a helpless invalid. Unable to continue her classes with the girls, she took on the ministry of Intercessory Prayer.

For the next ten years, Thomas Wintle was absorbed in developing outposts. He entrusted Pontnewydd to Mr. Hale and Cwmffrwdoer to Mr. Rolls. As the superintendent of the Mission, Mr. Wintle visited each of the outposts and felt that he needed a lady assistant, whose name was Miss Thornbury. It seems clear that, despite his absorption in social welfare, he still wanted an efficient house-to-house visiting system.

The time came when Wintle felt he needed someone else to help with visiting. So he decided wisely to appoint two Bible women, who quickly won the hearts of the housewives. One of his booklets described how the Bible women brought a woman called Mary and her husband to the Faith. Mary told her husband,

> "She was gentle and gracious to me. Before she left she read a few verses out of the Bible to me and knelt down and prayed. Oh! What a prayer! She didn't read out of a book but prayed from the heart for me to give my heart to Christ and be a good wife and mother. Tears were running down my cheeks. Then, Fred. She

prayed for you. 'But she has never seen me,' said Fred, 'So why should she pray for me?' Mary said, 'But she seems to know all about us and about our troubles. She prayed as though God was there by our side and was ready to answer anything. When she asked if she could come again, I told her you would like to see her.' Fred cried, 'Why did you say that? I don't want to see her, but she can come to see you.' Three months later Fred was a believer who was a loyal witness and who led others to Christ."

This personal evangelism was backed up by all-day prayer by intercessors, who often came away blessed and refreshed. Another kind of evangelistic outreach was the choice of strong volunteer men, who pushed a handcart through the estates. These were loaded with Christian booklets and New Testaments. A man called Joseph Beaupre continued this work up the valleys. Looking back over 40 years, Thomas Wintle wrote these words about his ministry.

"I have studiously avoided all sensational methods and all theatrical devices. I have not sought to attract the public, but to present Christ Crucified. In the morning service we read alternative verses. The evening is designed for the unconverted with attractive Gospel Songs. In the prayer room intercession was going on. Our ministry was clothing the naked, feeding the hungry, rescuing the perishing, visiting those in prison, comforting the sorrowing, strengthening the weak and cheering the faint."

In his later years, Thomas Wintle loved to walk through the trees by the Afon Lwyd and he carved on their trunks an ABC of Gospel texts. He received and prayed for reports of his helpers' works. He was honoured as sole Superintendent until his death in 1927. He had a supportive Council which included Lady Somerset, Mr. Cope-Morgan, who owned 'The Christian,' one surgeon and one solicitor. After his death, they decided to appoint a full-time minister, but the project was a failure and was handed over to local trustees. The outlying project ceased, but the central one continues to this day.

Cwmffrwdoer

In 1885, Mr. Wintle and his people opened a branch in their discarded iron hall. It was placed in the charge of Mr. Charles Rolls, who devoted many years to this work and to a small hall in George

Street in Pontypool. It was probably these Halls that were at Mr. Wintle's disposal when he dealt with the tragic results of two colliery disasters. Mr. Rolls was a miner and used his scanty leisure hours, when he was free, for what the press called 'a gracious Work.'

Pontnewydd Mission Hall

This Mission was planned by the Pontymoile Mission leaders as an extension to their outreach work. The Hall was the upper storey above a block of shops and was entered by a narrow staircase and a double door at the top. Its left side was kept for youth work and its right side for the worshippers. The Hall was very bare and there were only benches. Surprisingly enough, this Mission attracted many children. The whole work was entrusted to young Mr. Hales who dedicated himself to this task. It endured throughout his lifetime and for some time after the War. A journalist called 'Wanderer,' published in the Argus an account of his invitation visit. What he saw and heard remained unchanged for twenty years or so.

> "I found the Mission Hall, an oblong shaped room, some sixty foot long, occupied by about seventy improvised tables, with tin basins on them and rows of children, patiently waiting to be served with soup. The appetising odour filled the room and made me feel inclined to take my seat with the rest of the company. Bright, intelligent looking children, they were, with clean faces and hands, and though their clothing might not truthfully be termed respectable, yet it was palpable that their parents had sent them out as neatly dressed as circumstances would allow. It was not a dinner of waifs and strays, of ragged urchins and gutter children, such as we read of in our large towns, but it was a gathering as touching, aye, if not more so, than such a one.
>
> "The thought that these little boys and girls had all been brought up in good homes, with plenty of good food and clothes, and now were reduced to privation, was sufficient to make one sorrowful at heart. There is full sympathy for the honest, hardworking parents, who were forced to hear their children cry for food which they were unable to supply. 'Yes, sir,' said my guide as if interrupting my thoughts, 'They do look happy and comfortable now, but you should have seen them when they came to us first.'"

"Are all the children from Pontnewydd"? I asked, "No! There are a good many from Cwmbran and lower parts of Sebastopol." Meals were given every day to the children and, on Wednesdays, to the parents. In all 8,000 meals were given and gratefully received."

16 *Moral Crusades and Welfare Movements. 1885-1945*

This survey is devoted to a dozen or so Missions whose founding principles did not include overt evangelism nor spiritual growth nor increased interest in church life. They were essentially either rescue and welfare programmes or moral crusades. By far the oldest was the Seamen's Mission and the Railwaymen's Mission. They date back to the mid-nineteenth century and each was sponsored by philanthropists. Their only relevance to our subject is that some of its staff moved on to founding the other kind of Mission. This certainly happened at Barry and Cardiff dockland.

The Norwegian Church.

A remarkable offshoot was the rise of the Norwegian Church or Mission, which could cater for the needs of hundreds of seamen who brought in beams and props from Scandinavia to the Cardiff timber yards. In the days of furnaces and coalmines there was a constant demand for these. One could often see these crews on the streets, looking for drink and entertainment. The author of Cyfrol Goffa heard about one of these seamen who strayed into the Revival meetings, got very distressed and sat by the dock, thinking of taking his own life. The Norwegian Mission crossed the language barrier and reached his place of need. Principal Edwards heard about it and arranged for decent accommodation and companionship.

Rechabite Halls

A clearly moralist movement had been commenced by people,

who called themselves Rechabites, in memory of an Old Testament clan, who were forbidden all kinds of pleasure as proof of obedience to God. They were organised into tents called Hope, Peace, Faith, Grace, and their own buildings were shaped like Tents. There were loose links between the Tents at New Tredegar, Risca, Pontypool, Newport and Porth, Rhondda. In practice they stressed different dangers. The Tent, situated at Wintle's Mission in Pontypool, had leaders, who were almost obsessed with the drink problem and they made each new recruit sign a pledge of total abstention. They had a songbook called 'Crystal Springs' which went on and on about bright water streams, fresh fountains and other variants on the 'healthy water' theme.

Just to share a word about their hymnbooks, one section was devoted to marching songs such as this highly optimistic, even triumphal processional song, which was heard in the streets of Newport and Pontypool.

"A glorious day is dawning, a glorious light has burst
Hail the glorious Day of Gladness, Hallelujah let us sing.
Noble is our cause and righteous. On to Victory."

There were also special Welcome tunes about the need for uniting. Also there were several patriotic songs. The truly fascinating section consists of battle cries, "Begone strong drink! "Dash it down"! "When you see the ruddy wine." “Hooray for the sparkling water"! "Hail to the Crystal springs."

Though their ways were austere and high-minded, the Rechabite activities were full of fun and challenge. Only the sturdy Rechabite Hall at New Tredegar has stood up to heavy rumbling traffic. These Temperance Halls lost their vision and became all-age Social centres in the 1930's. The author remembers the last years at Charles Street Mission in Porth, where the social needs took prime place during the three great Depressions.

Forward Movement Mission Halls

The historians will have problems with the Forward Movement which was intended to be a series of interlocking Halls - Cardiff, Newport and Risca; Dowlais, New Tredegar and Pontypool; Porth, Neath and Swansea. They all differ in their development plans and some of them showed little sign of evangelism. One of the liveliest was at Dowlais and Penydarren where the community seemed to be transformed. On the other hand, the John Pugh memorial chapel at Porth did nothing. Malpas Road, Newport gradually became a more formal church but the one in East Newport was alive to people's needs. West Glamorgan gave belated support to the case for Port Talbot but by that time there was deep trouble and division, so much so that Mrs. Penn Lewis promoted a new work called a Christian Association for Women and Girls.

According to a South Wales Daily News report, Mrs. Penn Lewis had encouraged the good folk of Neath to set up a Mission Hall. This became her base of operations. There was a mini-revival in Neath in 1895 during which the Joshua brothers confessed their need for a deeper knowledge of the Lord. At Neath, both Frank and Seth did valuable soil-breaking work while continuing their itinerant work. Ten years later, Neath was rejoicing in its large Sunday school, its vigorous temperance movement, its rescue mission and other ventures.

The next step was to move on to Swansea but after that there was a slowing down of Mission expectations.

Oscar Snelling's Swansea Gospel Mission

This work began with the gift of land from Mrs. Rutter the Quakeress. Its first workers and faithful supporters were people, blessed in 1859, and anxious now to make intercession for their town. 'This supportive group had already sponsored a Ragged School in Back Street, so they had good premises for outreach work if they could find the right man. They didn't- but the Lord sent to them the one He had appointed.

After working in the South of England - applying George Muller's faith-principles to his own life, Oscar Snelling had been drawn towards the County Gospel Mission in Somerset and had built up his own team. He came to Swansea in 1865, supporting himself in some kind of printing work. Snelling recognised the hand of the Lord when someone offered him a set of large chambers. Meanwhile a final outbreak of the cholera scourge in the city sent many a frightened man or woman to seek salvation and to seek the Lord. They came along to the 'Place of Healing.' After Oscar Snelling entered the work, they were persuaded to engage in bolder ventures. For example, they booked the Royal Theatre for evangelistic meetings for seven years and then had to move to the Albert Hall, which was filled every day with responding people. All this convinced the town's religious leaders that they ought to give open support, not opposition. It seems that the high spot of each year was the Watch-night Service when hundreds responded in an act of confession.

At the start of this century the Mission became absorbed in social problems and devised more schemes of practical work such as hospital services or the Voluntary Probation Service. Mr. Snelling himself was a member of the Board of Guardians, he was never short of helpers and seemed able to communicate his own sunny spirit to his teams. He was always heard humming, 'Be Glad in the Lord and Rejoice.'

The impression given in their official history was that the Oscar Snelling Mission was identified only with a set of rooms in Orchard Street. The Rev. Seth Joshua was still pleading with them, as late as 1925, to erect a Memorial Building. The entire Lord's Day "private" services were conducted in a Hall or Room in High Street.

It would seem that evangelistic mission and God-given revivals can complement one another but can never be mixed up, so the great national Revival of 1904-5 scarcely touched Town Missions. Only the Branches such as Old Bridge Street were aware of it.

Pontymoile Mission and its Contribution to Social Welfare

Thomas Wintle was a native of Abersychan and a worker at Siemen's in Blaenavon. He was married to the master-roller's daughter. The young and clever metal engraver was a natural manager and was sent to Siemen's works in Swansea. During his stay there he got caught up in the Revival and yielded his life to Christ as a witness. His first activities were as a leader of the anti-alcohol movement. He became a sworn enemy of intemperance. When he returned to Pontypool, he set up a Ragged School in the estate yard. He also welcomed and encouraged the Rechabite Movement and organised the Blue Ribbon Society.

There was also a little preaching centre in a hut. From about 1880 to 1900, he did work as an evangelist, but the death of his wife upset him and all the work she had developed in the home, Bethany, was suspended. Much of the work was left to Mr. Hale in Pontnewydd and Mr. Rolls in Cwmynyscoy. Unfortunately, his own health could not stand the strain. In 1883, he invited a trained worker called Miss Thornbury, to be a Bible woman, visiting every house. In about 1889, they planned to build a purpose-built Hall with a reading room and a recreation room, also a Coffee Club, library and soup kitchen. Later, a dormitory was added, with a special washroom for travellers.

Figure 23: Pontymoile Mission Hall was used for young people's rehabilitation

His preaching centre was simply a large stone on the roadside opposite the tavern in Cwmynyscoy. Crowds gathered to listen to his passionate Gospel preaching. On land, leased by the Hanbury family, they now erected a purpose-built building, which continued until 1996.

This social and rescue work took up time and resources. The magistrates, at the Monday Court, would put young offenders on remand, on condition that they were under the supervision of Clarke and Wintle. Many became believers and the rest became useful members of society.

Wintle was a man of sanctified common sense and a man of great compassion. He developed a wonderful flair for writing booklets with dramatic titles such as 'Ben the Prize Fighter;' 'Tom Jones the Bailer;' 'The Pauper;' 'The Witches Curse;' 'A Lump of Pudding;' 'A Bit of Blue.' 'Through Death to Life' and 'Heaven's Telephone.' The stories are based on the ventures of some of their lodgers. These passers-by, tramps, tinkers, packmen and runaways were not only given soup but a bed in a dormitory. A good example will be Winnie Smith wrote a poem about her adventures.

> "I remember that, when I was desperate I walked from Abertillery over the mountain, seeking a new home. It was the Mission that gave me food and clothing and took a friendly interest in me. I came to know the Lord Jesus as my Saviour and I worked willingly for the Mission. I moved back to Abertillerv, brought up a family and then moved back to Pontymoile, where I became caretaker."

Winnie looked after the Mission Hall for many years after her husband died. After her death, they found this little poem hidden away in the caretaker's rooms.

"Ere long, I found my Saviour with joy,
Who guided and waited over me.
His song since then my tongue employ
In grateful fervent melody."
So here I am glad to say
Loved, cared for and befriended
Intending to stay unless sent away,
Till my journey here is ended"

Another rescued character was Tom Phillips who became the secretary of the 'Blue Ribbon' while still in the army.

Wintle also got involved in labour relations from time to time and acted as a peacemaker. Wintle's next objective was the education of adults. He called for the appointment of volunteer men who would push a Gospel handcart around the streets. Joseph Beaupre took a handcart up through the valleys. Wintle was given a Bible carriage to do such work, which went on late into the night. Distribution of scriptures became the top priority. But Thomas Wintle still kept his preaching spot and stall in the Market Place near the travelling theatre and just below where the Bethel Mission was built. He was admired for his visiting of the widows and children after the

Llanerch disaster of 1890

Thomas Wintle remained sole Superintendent until his death in 1927, but he had a supportive council which included Lady Somerset, R. Cope-Morgan, who owned 'The Christian' and one surgeon and one solicitor. After his death, a body of trustees decided to appoint a full-time minister. But the project was a failure. The entire project was handed over to local trustees who were also members. They relinquished the four offshoots one by one, leaving the central building with its massive care and welfare facilities. (1935-1940).

Perhaps our society does not need the Snellings, the Pughs, the Gwythers or the Wintles any longer. Is it the case that our cosy culture has less time and concern for the dropouts and the wanderers.

17 *Advance of the Gospel Halls on the Coast*

Barry Gospel Mission

The first large urban area since Bridgend was part of the same busy coal port as Cadoxton where the three freight railways from the mines and stone quarries came together. Whereas Cardiff had its large Seamen's Mission and small Railwaymen's, Barry and Cadoxton already had a large mid-nineteenth century Railwaymen's' Mission and a small Seamen's Mission. Both Gospel-preaching groups had born fruit and slowly evolved into the Barry Gospel Mission (an embryonic Church). It employed a full time Missioner from 1901-1916. After his day, Mr. Heycock and David Newton provided the ministry. Again in 1932, when Pastor Harrison left, his place was taken by an evangelist named Parsons who came in from the 'Sailors Rest' in Barry Dock. Those links with the Railwaymen's and Seamen's Missions were broken eventually.

This work was blessed, between the two World Wars, with two unusually gifted ministers. First came Ivor Powell the evangelist and personal worker who had that knack of discerning any soul in distress and confusion. He would win their complete trust and show them the way to the place of God's mercy. The most dramatic examples of changed personalities are exhibited in a book entitled 'We Saw it Happen.' Never did the tongue of criticism lash Ivor Powell as his story-telling fascinated the listeners. After he went away on his World Mission, the leaders drew a deep breath and called another Barry Bible College student, who provided them with richest fare.

Frail in his frame and limited in bodily vigour, Paul Tucker knew no limit to his anointing as a Bible teacher. In his student days, almost sixty years, ago the author heard him preaching deeply from the truths in Psalm 139. The theme was about Gods Four Attributes. In his mature years, Paul Tucker also had the ability to expose the defects in the cruder forms of destructive criticism of the Scriptures and fashionable doubts about doctrine. Men like him could well have prepared Wales for another great post-war Revival.

During the sixties under the ministry of Rev Kenneth Peel, the Barry Gospel Mission evolved into what is now the Princes Street Evangelical Church.

Wilberforce Hall

This was one of the special interests of de Courcy Hamilton who insisted on open membership and officially used the Book of Common Prayer, alongside Mission Hymnbooks, There was progress during ex-missionary Rev. Harry Ackland's two years. Then came B. S. Fidler who didn't like this compromise policy. He and his students favoured the Luchana Mission Hall instead, so the gap between the two Missions widened, especially when Hamilton died. By 1945, the Hall had 24 members, which dropped further until the Rev. John Cook arrived. Some members of Wilberforce Hall took a 'positive' interest in the work of evangelists such as Duncan, but the truth is that Wilberforce inherited the spirit of Revival rather than its practical outworking.

Luchana Mission, Cadoxton

This was one of three Missions opened by de Courcy Hamilton after his return from Spain. He was deeply concerned with the condition of the navvies and stevedores and we were told that sometimes he would invite such men from the new freight line behind his mansion and allow them to enter the magnificent Scandinavian Hall - removing their heavy boots first. His wife had helped run a Mission for Excavators and when she died, the bereaved husband built Luchana Mission in her honoured memory. He personally invited the Rev. B.S. Fidler to take charge of Luchana, which included the training of evangelists and the Barry Bible School of Evangelism.

This rather reserved businessman discovered that the rambling building, designed to be a hotel, was not going to open because the buyer could not get a drink licence. Mr. Fidler and his 'boys' repaired, redecorated and refurbished the big chambers. Gradually it became more of a resource centre than a College. Hall and College together could man beach Missions, run open-air meetings, help the resident colporteur and so on. After the training was over, many went off to the toughest places as pastors. These workers could count on faithful prayer and even the financial support of Luchana. The removal of the Bible College to Bridgend has put an end to all such links. Praise God for De Courcy Hamilton, this steward who faithfully used his wealth.

B. S. Fidler served these ventures until the sixties but the little white-haired man with a white moustache and fiery eyes was seen and heard no more. Colportage work, with or without the Gospel Caravan, continued up to the outbreak of the war. As for the Beach Missions run by Luchana Mission Hall and the Bible College, they never gave up their annual witness on the sands.

Penarth and Dinas Powys

There is no evidence of a Mission or children's work in this wealthy upper class Plassey street fellowship. A more active Brethren-style group had its Mission in Cogan near the railway complex, but has moved the greatest activity much nearer Dinas Powys.

City of Cardiff

The peculiarity of Cardiff is that most of the Mission work grew around the three main Brethren movements, two of which had seceded from the Bible Christian Church. Of the five earliest ones, scattered around the Dockland suburbs, we have found detailed reports of Clive Hall, Adamstown and Ebenezer. Since the war, they have grown and total about twenty in the one city. We will focus upon three of the early nineteenth century groups, each of which seemed unaffected by the currents of revival. Perhaps they were too Anglicised; perhaps their new mode of worship could not be made to mix with their old forms.

At the east end of the city was a Mission Hall, called Eastmoor, which seems to have vanished altogether. It is on the list of the Forward Movement and must have served the needs of the first housing estates, east of the Rhymney.

Heath Gospel Hall

This cause started in a house in 1915. The present secretary, Mr. Turner, insists that the Hall was completely autonomous from the beginning. In fact a witness had begun in Russell Street as open-air meetings only. Then they found a room for Sunday school work and Gospel meetings in Tavistock Street and they named it the Welcome Mission Hall. The third and final move was to Curll Avenue. The actual Hall was set up in 1920, at the commencement of a decade of expansion. Certain people from Mackintosh Hall helped to set it up.

Towards the end of that fruitful period, the young people were encouraged to go, after Church, to the Turner house for singing and coffee. The Mission Hall also developed Children's Meetings, but the main effort concentrated on the '6.30 crusade.' The Mission always had its own list of approved preachers and every one of these was expected to challenge the audience to make a personal acceptance of Christ as Saviour. About 30 people were involved, but the number of workers has diminished. Only two of the pioneers are still alive. They are Mr. and Mrs. Hannay, who are now in their nineties.

Upper Clive Street Mission, with Windsor Hall

This work began when several pilots in Cardiff Docks were converted at the Seamen's Mission. Their first fellowship meetings were in a room over some offices in Stuart Street, close to the Pierhead. They moved on to a large upper room in the eighties, built over a stable in Eleanor Place, which they called the 'Seamen's Bethel.' They appointed their own Missioner and Colporteur who converted a dozen more pilots and boatmen. The earliest known leaders were Peter Evans, William Gould, and William Howe, who took charge of the Sunday school. His constant challenge to the youngsters, who asked too many questions, was "What is that to thee? Follow thou Me!"

Another little branch was set up in Thorney Loft, writes veteran

Mr. Fish. It was this one in Grangetown that moved to Windsor Hall, under the leadership of Buck the schoolmaster. Many were converted through the testimony of the sisters in their own meeting also.

Round about 1899, new halls were set up, such as Ebenezer Hall, Adamstown, and Mackintosh Place. Mr. Fish said that there was a happy Christian spirit and a willingness to use their trades to improve the work, such as blacksmith, plumber and shipwright. They made their own chairs and benches. One group excavated a Baptistry in their own grounds.

Generally speaking the Gospel Halls preferred the usual forms of evangelism such as open conferences. From about 1910 onwards, they developed Missionary links with work in Central Africa. Eventually, their Brethren magazine, 'Echoes of Service' (BATH), handled missionary gifts and 'applications to serve',

Some of the young men formed teams, preaching in the Caerphilly and Rhymney Valley areas. Others specialised in children's work using their halls for events for the poor children. It is said that one of those halls alone could hold 290 children. Windsor hall was a smaller Hall. It had a small desk, a stove in the centre and a lamp in the doorway. The first conferences were held in Windsor Hall until about 1940. Windsor Hall's leaders were Thomas Hall, James Buck, Charles Buck, Edward Edwards and George Elliot, whose wife was famed in Cardiff City as a needle worker.

The last leader was James Shannon, who had the sad task of removing the remains of a bombed out hall and transferring members to the nearby Grangetown brotherhood. Plans were made to extend the work at Clive St., which stood on waste ground known as 'Jenny Ball's' ditch. We should mention that, in its last years, it had a Sunday school, led by Brother Heaven and a weeknight fellowship.

The format of Clive Street services was a Bible Study and a Lord's Day Service, i.e. Breaking of Bread, the afternoon Sunday school and the evening visits to lodging houses. A small kitchen was set up for supplying stew for impoverished Irish women.

> "It was a never-to-be-forgotten sight to see these Irish women, broken down under the power of the Gospel. It developed into a Mothers' Meeting and a Sewing Meeting, knitting socks for the soldiers."

The women members had much more influence after the men went to the War. Seven remaining teachers, from Windsor Road, asked to become full members and asked to be permitted to share in the Breaking of Bread. It was this combined group which was able to pay for a proper Gospel Hall.

The new Hall accommodated 100 upstairs and 50 downstairs. It had a pulpit and proper chairs. There was a separate room for the Band of Hope, Christian Endeavour and the Bible Class, taught by Mrs. Hart. All the meetings used Alexander's Hymns. As in other Missions, there was only a morning Collection. They must have had a Statement of Faith and a Roll of Membership. They had never had a Pastor or Minister and they have never affiliated with any other Evangelical group in Wales. Somehow the waves of Revival 1904-24 passed them by, even when Revival Meetings were being held a few hundred yards away.

Ebenezer Gospel Hall 1899

The record of 50 years shows a continuous and confident experience of God's help and guidance. This has encouraged the surviving members to hold fast. It began in 1870 with a Seamen's Mission in a ship called 'Thisbe' in the West Dock. During that Mission, several channel pilots, boatmen and dockers came to Christ and were changed and became full of the 'Joy of the Forgiven.'

Some of the converts held a Gospel Meeting every Sunday night on the Pierhead. Crowds listened to testimonies. Mr. Gale, their Bible teacher, hired a room in Stuart Street and rented rooms in Eleanor Place. These included a large preaching Room and smaller rooms downstairs, where the Prayer and Bible meetings were held. Soon there were enough children to hold a Sunday school, so Peter Evans hired a Sunday school room in Harrowby Street near the old sea lock, known locally as Auntie Ann's. This became the centre for the Women's Work, including a Garment Class. Next, they purchased two houses in Evelyn Street. It was here that guest speakers, including George Muller, came to speak. Two more Bible Teachers came. It is said that they travelled by ferry to Penarth. That Hall lasted 25 years and was replaced, on October 5th.1899, by Ebenezer Hall.

Figure 24: Ebenezer Gospel Hall, Cardiff

They also compiled an Assembly Register and established a Board of Trustees. Visitors called it a 'white elephant,' but soon it was quite full. The main Hall accommodated 500 people and had side classrooms and a basic schoolroom. There were many baptisms in this exciting period and a constant stream of admissions to the Sunday school. Curiously enough, the entire School was run by seven men. There were faithful teachers, such as Mr. Lewis Jones, for 30 years and Miss Jeffrey, for 53 years.

Ebenezer became the host for Missionary conferences, the most celebrated speaker of which was Mr. Dan Crawford from 'Darkest Africa.' Ebenezer also launched the Grangetown 'Open Air and

Tract Band,' guided by Mr. Desallioud. During the Depression years Mr. Dalling ran a soup kitchen and arranged for a speaker every day. Another small initiative was a Sunday school, held in shop premises in Stuart Street, belonging to Mr. Westerman. Despite many discouragements, it developed a very large Sunday school and the shop was slightly adapted. Two years later, some of the leaders erected a wooden building out at Leckwith and this was where they finally built a Mission hall.

Even in the wartime there were constant rescue and care activities. On one memorable night in January 1941, their Hall was occupied. A Sunday school tea party was scrapped because 100 evacuated people were directed to sleep there. One leader, Mr Groves, saw this as an opportunity to hold short Gospel services, such as the one on 'fleeing to the Rock.' More recently it has co-operated with Clive St. and Windsor Gospel Hall, which had been transferred to a rented chapel in Paget Street, when a bomb had demolished their own building. The account ends with their own favourite verse:-

"His Love in times past forbids us to think,
He'll leave us at last, in trouble to sink;
Each sweet Ebenezer we have in review,
Confirms His good pleasure to help us right through."

Mackintosh Hall

In 1885, some young men from Adamstown acquired a shop on the corner of Miskin Street and turned it into a Gospel Hall. In 1890 they moved to Richmond Hall at the top end of Richmond Road. It was much larger but the people in the meetings could hear what was going on in the stables down below them. The local families who joined this assembly wanted a Sunday school for their children and expected a number of conversions. They erected Mackintosh Hall in 1897, when a March of Witness was arranged as a celebration. A graph in the Church records, shows the membership climbing from 220, in October 1904, to 350, in 1923. Yet, there is no proof whatsoever of responses to the Welsh Revival.

This Hall, which later included two houses was very spartan, with scrubbed floorboards, squares of linoleum and hot air gratings. Without curtains, it was so hot in the Summer that they turned on the fans. During a conference, the upstairs balcony could be opened.

There were Gospel Missions every year, either in a tent or a general building. They visited every house and distributed the 'Emergency Post.' Between 1920 and 1940 there was a Tract Band, who stood outside, giving out booklets and invitations to Gospel Services. Singing was first used in 1919 in the evening meetings and was led by a man with a tuning fork. The Sunday school had 80 infants alone. The school hall was the scene of annual singing and reciting programmes for the parents and this feature greatly increased the numbers of children between the Wars. All children and youth instruction was Bible-based. The Junior Covenanters had two groups and there have been annual associated Camps. Finally, Mackintosh Hall's Missionary vision and commitment has sent 20 Missionaries to various countries.

They set up six branches. Wyvern Road Mission, which included open-air work and weeknight girls' class for needlework. They all moved to Fitzroy Street Mission in Jan. 1931. This, converted, became a centre for evangelism. Tavistock Street (1910) became the Welcome Hall. The Heath Gospel Hall. See above (1915 and 1920), Bethesda Gospel Hall in Rhiwbina. (1930). Work was started in Penylan in 1925, but this became Minster Gospel Hall in a new building, off Newport Road, in October 1927. Finally, at Taff's Well in 1920, a tent campaign became a Gospel Hall called Glanllyn.

Town of Newport

This town had its own mixture of Mission Halls and Gospel Halls. There were Five Brethren Missions in the town centre, which varied considerably in their aims and activities. The best known of these was Mount Joy Hall, which definitely had Sunday school and children's meetings before the last War. There was little specific effort to evangelise adults, but one member, Mr. John Capper commenced popular meetings during the last year of the War.

In a side street leading off Stow Hill opposite the Cathedral there was the Exclusive Brethren's place of Assembly. This was always secretive, leaving all its affairs to the elders. Very strict rules governed daily conduct and relationships. There's no evidence of outgoing Mission.

Maindee Cottage Gospel Mission

The exact opposite was Maindee Cottage Gospel Mission, built in the 1890s in Probate Place which organised as much outreach work as possible and also provided services to the hospitals. This was the second Mission Hall to be built by a Mr Walter Purnell who had previously been with the Salvation Army. The Hall untypically had only 40 seats. This congregation was very laid back, having no hymn book, communion table, bible class, membership roll, statement of faith, Band of Hope, Christian Endeavour, Gideons, but there was a Sunday school. Breaking of bread was first attempted in 1940. Unsurprisingly they did not send out any missionaries. There were many restrictions on the role of women.

The whole fellowship had a strong emphasis on simplicity, appealing to the common man. They were not linked to anyone else's assemblies. The only known pastor was Walter Pennel who initially held meetings in a front room in Livingstone Place. It is now under the control of a special Trust.

Crindau Gospel Chapel

This fellowship, now known as Crindau Gospel Church was established in March 1901in the Shaftesbury area of Newport. Its position, above a main street row of shops, made it possible to reach many disadvantaged children and youths from the streets that then existed behind them. The fellowship of this 200-seat hall with a pulpit had a membership role, made use of the Authorised version of the Bible and used Sankeys hymns. A week night Bible Class was attended by about 40 people and took a conversational form. Women only took part in teaching Sunday school classes, which had strong attendance. For the breaking of bread, seats were arranged around the communion table and various prayers and portions of scripture were shared, often extending to an hour of open worship. All finance was collected from freewill offering. This mission hall supported two missionaries – Mildred Wilkes (Japan) and Anne Ellis (Kenya)

Other Halls in Newport

Vine Street Mission has a puzzling history. A former member spoke of the restrictions, for example, on cosmetics, cinemas, dances, fancy hairdos and jewellery. First impressions of their hall were that they were closed in. Nevertheless, a few elderly men remember how the group took tracts and gospels all around the neighbourhood.

Incidentally, the Nant Coch Mission came late in the day. Its first members were drawn from the Christians who attended a House meeting in Fields Park. Nant Coch is situated in the midst of the prosperous business community.

Pentecostal Missions were rare and were not called Halls. The East Newport one is called a Church and can still be seen in Rockfield Street. The West Newport one is called a Temple, which, for some years before the War, was under the care of Pastor Edward Jeffreys and Matthew Francis. Just after the war the fellowship moved to Stow Hill but it was definitely a church and not a Mission.

The last category of Mission Hall was inspired and organised by individuals and each one was clearly intended to evolve into a Church. Thomas Delahay, a railway constructor, working for Pooleys, persuaded the local people to develop Nash Mission, which became a great success. Next he persuaded the Usk Road Chapel to sponsor a Mission Hall on a new housing estate in Liswerry in 1888. It was called a Mission/School/Hall and it filled with children and parents by the year of the Welsh Revival. Things looked promising for twenty years under self- sacrificing leaders. Delahaye stayed on as pastor from 1886-1906.

A much younger man, Augustus Purnell, formed a Mission Hall in Corporation Road. This began with children's meetings in a wainwright's shop. Its first wood and zinc chapel is still visible. Four Purnells were involved in this Mission outreach. It met a community need and grew swiftly for at least thirty years before it evolved. It is said that their first communion or breaking of bread was decided upon suddenly without benefit of service book.

The most publicised of all these mission style fellowships were set up by Mr. Pardoe Thomas. The Commercial Road Baptist church was in its prime and had enough resources to have Spurgeon preaching there twice. However, Mr. Pardoe Thomas fell out with the church administrators 111 went off to a new base. They had to use four temporary premises before they settled down, They had a centre in Alexandra Road and a relief centre in Dolphin Street. Pardoe Thomas's father offered them part of his sailmaking and repair shop in Alma Street and this is where they met to read God's Word, to pray, to sing the Songs of Zion and to hear expository addresses. There was no roll, but each member made a private covenant with the Lord. What makes Newport so complicated, is that many Mission halls changed their names and meeting places.

From Newport to Chepstow by Coastal Routes

There were only the Railway Missions at Undy and Sudbury at work in propagating the Gospel. Products of these Missions played a significant part in the Welsh Revival. A different group representing Llanvaches and Magor masterminded the Penhow Mission Hall (1909). It defined its beliefs as Calvinist Baptist and always insisted on baptism by immersion. The rules demanded regular communion services around their 'Coronation Table.' At the bi-annual church meeting, all affairs were conducted in strict confidentiality and the men and women were treated equally. A special collecting bag was used to support the cause and to maintain one missionary - Mary Parsons. It had its own secretary but no deacons probably because it was under the close scrutiny of the two senior churches. Its whole life has been uneventful. Leaders and Bible class teachers were Mr. Harris, Mr. Humphrey, Mr. Smith and Mr. White. Apathy and slow decline has weakened the cause but Sunday school work flourished a little longer.

Underwood

What a strange story this Mission could tell. A young student pastor, Dennis Monger, worked the district in 1949. He saw this dismantled prisoner-of-war camp inside barbed wire. He saw the sturdy Nissen huts, the breeze block ex-canteens, the rusty fittings and the weed covered sites. Undismayed by all this, Dorothy and Dennis moved into primitive rooms alongside seventy families who needed a visitor and counsellor. Children's meetings had been assigned to an old Ablution hut. Despite all this change, Mr. Monger persuaded the Council to provide him with two or three outbuildings, so the gospel hall took shape all through 1950. The rest of its story is outside the sphere of this survey. Their motto is still 'All one in Christ Jesus.' Surely it was amongst the last fruit from the Mission Hall tree.

Figure 25: Underwood Sunday School

18 *Missions in Powys*

One would think there were enough tiny chapels in the four valleys north and west of Pontrilas to meet every need, yet people still built mission halls. The two Grosmont Missions were virtually on the border between Gwent and Powys. The local press noticed the advent and growth of the large Sunday school and children's work. Such work was transferred in two groups. One met above the Town Hall; the other met in its own Mission Hall at the top of the lane towards Pontrilas. The only surviving members today are the Jobsons who used to travel up from Hereford. The town mission developed children's work, but the other one had quiet meetings rather like Quaker meetings, with readings but no sermons or talks.

There were glowing reports of revival meetings at nearby Norton. Ten miles west of Grosmont you will find three little Mission Halls, on the West Side of the old Hereford to Abergavenny drovers' road.

Llanwenarth Breast

One of the most interesting experiences was the discovery of a tiny chapel on the sunlit Sugarloaf slopes. After a splendid tea, we viewed a building down the bottom of a steep slope. The first suggestion of a worship site came from Rev. Cook of Frogmore Street. A Mrs, Williams volunteered the use of her large house.

A very interesting Hall had been built by a smallholder on Llanwenarth Breast on his own property for the sake of the mountain people, who were members of Glangwrney, down below. The building is still in use, even though the steep access would sorely test elderly people today.

Pantygelli

Pantygelli Evangelical Mission Hall is on the old drovers' road from Abergavenny to Hereford. The origin of worship had long since been forgotten, but one local family claim that converted local believers met in a nearby farmhouse. Deeds show that it was acquired by the Y.M.C.A from the trustees in 1926, when several denominations were being urged to do something for the hundreds of youths left idle because of the Depression. When those bad days were over it was likely that idle young men disappeared into trenches and tanks, local people returned to Mission work fetching children from the mountain villages. If there was children's weeknight work in that Hall they would have walked along a public footpath through the lush meadows. Lanes also led up to quarry cottages and to smallholdings. Only a few elderly ladies, who have difficulty in keeping it in good repair, now use the Hall. Every Sunday a few ladies still meet there to worship on their own.

Llanellen

Here, there was some kind of Hall meeting in this pleasant village, west of Abergavenny. Llanellen is not far from Bailey Glas Cottage, close to the Usk, where a small prayer fellowship met at the turn of the century. There were meetings in a large house at or near Llanellen thirty years later, but no Mission Hall was formed.

Penybont

On the eastern hills near Llandrindod and Builth, there was a little chapel, called Penybont, an old Welsh Calvinist Methodist centre. There was also a Quaker worship place, called The Pales that had existed for over two hundred years in total independence. The one person who had a vision for this forgotten area was J. O. Jenkins, the magistrate, who must have sent an appeal to the 'Revival centres' in South Wales. Meanwhile the small local group of 'Children of the Revival' went on interceding for their families and neighbours. Among these was a young farmer who returned full of fire, from revival meetings in South Wales. He failed to get from his Vicar any encouragement or permission. They could not have the Parish Hall so the forty-four people impressed by the young farmer's words about praying for neighbours and friends, moved to a house or farmhouse at Dolau. This was in February 1905. Presumably it was this nucleus which brought Anglicans and Methodists together eventually in Cregrina where they prayed for revival.

George and Stephen Jeffreys arrived almost two years later on January 11th.1907. The crowds started to come from the farm-steads once the people had heard of these two dynamic men. They had responded to their preaching and teaching, even more so after they heard the news of wonderful healings. A Press reporter has set these mass public meetings in the old Quaker meeting place, but that would have been impossible in February on the Radnorshire moors, where you could not stand for hours inside or outside an unheated building. No! The main public meetings were held in that main road Calvinist Methodist chapel until it, too, was overflowing and they had to use nearby fields, when weather permitted and in a farm field in the spring. They came from the farms from over thirty miles away, so room and fodder had to be found for many horses.

George and Steven the Jeffreys brothers, themselves, used the other little Quaker room at the edge of the spa town called Llandrindod Wells for intercession and for dealing with 11 precious souls. It was probably, when they were in that room, that crippled Edith Carr came and asked for laying-on of hands and was healed. There was excitement over at Penybont when she stepped forward to testify to her healing and then promised to accompany all the singers with her 'new hands given by God.' There is a strong belief, in that area, that Evan Roberts visited briefly in February 1906 - including Cregrina - in his travels. But he was in a Conference at Bangor in North Wales in March 1906, Llandeilo in April, Leicester in May and Keswick, Cumberland, in July, 1906.

Dolau

An English visitor noticed the absence of any urging or pressurising at these Missions as long as the hearers confessed Christ freely. Altogether, there were fifty-seven converts in 1907, but the Jeffreys could never forget that first miraculous healing. At this stage, healings were considered to be extra blessings whilst the real commission to preach the Gospel counted far more. This is the local correspondent's version of developments there.

> "From the first time I saw them, I was much impressed with their earnest manner, and we felt they were men with a special message, given them by God to deliver. They do not press people to

respond to the invitation to pray or give. They only say that if any will take part they shall be blessed in doing so. At the end of the meeting there is no urging of people to go to the front or to an enquiry room. Mr George Jeffreys, who usually speaks first, is a fluent speaker with a good delivery, intensely in earnest. Stephen gets up after a chorus and prays with what a wonderful power. There were six definite conversions on Tuesday night."

Another reporter said he was "struck by Stephen's frankness and joyousness and wondered why he protested that he was not a preacher, but a deliverer of what he was taught from God's word and prompted by the Spirit to declare." Such language seemed strange to him.

It is probable that the little Mission in Duck Lane, Builth Wells, was a by-product of this work. It did not flourish in the same way as the Cregrina Mission. East of Llandrindod, there were few enduring effects other than at Dolau on the moors and Coxall, on the far side of Knighton, which was visited, in 1906, by a Miss Richards - claimed by the local paper to be a follower of Evan Roberts.

Cregrina Mission Hall

This began with the purchase of a property from Mr. Charles Evans, the blacksmith, and the costs were borne by farmers Davies, Fronolau, Watkins, Pentwyn, Gittoes of Helyg Farm, James Griffiths of Rhos, William Phillips and William Protheroe. It was agreed that the hall would be available for all denominations and it soon became evident that Anglicans, annoyed by the Vicar's dictatorial attitude, would also join them in an acceptable form of service, which combined ancient ceremonial with free spiritual praises.

A group of converts lived on these hilltop farms. Leading men and women went ahead in faith to create the Cregrina Mission in a centre, which Methodists also used. From time to time, the local press recorded special Mission Services, a Young People's Crusade (Mr. Bennett) and visits from gifted Bible-teachers from the first Conventions arranged by Mr. J.O. Jenkins.

The pioneers transformed what looked like a large village cottage, by knocking down the interior walls to make room for fifty to sixty people. Veterans still remember the open fire grate, the oil lamps for lighting, the hard wooden chairs and the old harmonium.

After some years it was only the Methodist Sunday school, which used it along with the 'Keswick' group. After 1931, the Baptists from Franksbridge chapel used it for a monthly service after they lost their meeting at Glanedw, where they used to baptise and meet for worship.

Figure 26: Cregrina Rural Mission Hall

These services were the first to be conducted by ministers. 'Cregrina' proved to be a spiritual refuge and was careful to respect both Anglican and Nonconformist traditions. The Methodists withdrew altogether in 1965 after which Cregrina was formally renamed as Cregrina Free Mission and was opened as such by the Rev. Hywel Griffiths in 1966. Four members of the Evans family undertook responsibility thirty years ago.

Steadily this work has grown until today as new families arrive. That tree which God had planted will never die and many have come to personal salvation through the faithful teaching of the

Word. The cottage/Mission Room has been redecorated and refurbished but never substantially changed. It has enjoyed splendid guest speakers such as the Keswick in Wales convention speakers. There is a 25 member congregation out there on the moors, and there is a good Sunday school. One dedicated servant of the Lord, Charles Evans, the founder's son, and his talented wife have been its sponsors and they have given faithful support over the years. But they would say, "God is faithful! To God be the glory!"

Figure 27: Opening of Cregrina Mission

Ackhill Hall

This is close to the border with Herefordshire. Even in 1899, the

Christian groups living at Upper Dolau Farm and down in Presteigne desired a meeting place. The project was held up by a local landowner whose widow, the dynamic Mrs. Stephens, eventually gave enough land for a Hall and a school. Another notable lady, Miss Passey, who had been blessed at South Wales revival meetings, promised generous financial support. So this building project was completed in August 1905 - in record time.

The Hall was opened on 25th, August 1905, when one hundred people heard Rev. D.H. Jenkins speak of the true church of Christ. One month later, formal membership was set up and a church covenant imparted "following which, time was spent in prayerful preparation as they felt that, without the Lord's sealing and blessing, all would be in vain." Baptisms took place in the River Lugg and at least twelve were added. They called Arthur Derman to be pastor but they could not provide enough means or accommodation for long.

Many Bible College students have been invited to their first pastorates there, but some were not invited to stay on. Some of R. B. Jones' Bible Institute's best students came there, such as Alex Leach, Stanley Jackson, Cyril Evans the poet and Mr. Beechey who gave sound evangelical teaching and Bible-based instruction, wherever they were accepted. The Ackhill pastorates lasted about five years each but there is one tragic exception. Llewelyn Beechey came from the Porth Bible Institute where he trained hard for the work that lay ahead. Alas! He did not live out his five years and it was left to his family to serve Ackhill church under later pastorates, even when it was temporarily joined to the Baptist Union. His son, Peter, has continued to serve here. The story of Ackhill is a constant reminder how the Lord can use the gifted and the wealthy and the dreamers of dreams as well as faithful stewards to accomplish His hidden purposes in a place where one would not expect a plenteous harvest.

19 *Small Springs in North Wales*

There is no sign of a Mission in the upper Severn Valley nor the Tanat valley although the Rev. Joseph Jenkins, Miss Florrie Evans, Miss Rosina Davies and the Rev. H. Hughes had held Revival meetings. In the Welsh-speaking churches the converts stayed in the fold, but in the Anglicised districts there were fellowships meeting at or near Ruabon, (the Powell Parry group is better remembered as Plas Bennion). Also they met at some villages north of Wrexham, where the Rev. J. Ellis Jones tried to apply the truths, taught by his hero, R. B. Jones, in the glorious 1905 –1909 preaching festivals. There were teams of witness, but few Mission Halls here.

A visiting preacher, Rev. A.H. Roberts wrote for the 'Cardigan and Teifiside Advertiser,' a number of impressions of the long-term effects of Revival. He attended one of those weeknight fellowships, which still met as late as 1939,

> "I remember a strange night in a little chapel in North Wales, with only young people there. A number of us went out to hold a prayer meeting at the house of an unbeliever. The rest stayed behind to pray. Then, I heard a little boy, running home from the meeting to call out, "Mam! The whole Chapel is full of angels." In the 'big seat,' a young man was standing, dumbfounded with a Bible in front of him, at the story of the Cross. He had had a vision of Christ and that lit up the meeting. It was hard to bring it to an end as the young people went on testifying."

Another man from Ruabon told how, at first, he had preferred W. S. Jones's Bible meditations and R.B. Jones's expositions to the passionate utterances of other preachers. Gradually, however, as Mr. Powell Parry predicted, these sessions were used to denounce other movements, especially those that were used to oppose the Word of God. The more charismatic types of believer moved on to other kinds of Church.

A picture is slowly emerging of two or three Mission Halls inside the great northern bend of the River Dee. At the start of the last war, three ladies came to seek refuge in Llangollen. They attended a Forward Movement owned chapel in Brook Street, which was decaying by 1939. In a time of prayer, they realised that the Lord had a plan for them to continue the witness. They even had an English language Mission called Penllyn. So the Mission came into being and lasted their whole life-time.

We have a description of the Penllyn building from a Mr. Jim Harding, who visited the building in the early 1960's. He was told that it had been taken over by the Forward Movement sometime after the 1904 Revival. It was a chapel building not a Hall. There were 75 seats, an organ, a traditional pulpit and a communion table. There were no vestries downstairs, but there was an upstairs room, which would be used for their Bible Class. There was freedom for women to take part in prayer, teaching and testimony. The witness was kept up for 40 years.

Somehow, the fire had died down in Clwyd by the nineteen twenties but few attempts were made to set up Mission Halls on the Ruabon to Mold road, there appeared little Missions, such as Adwy and Rockwood. Adwy has lasted right down to today under its ordained ministers.

Rockwood Mission

This Mission on the edge of the moors, began life in a cottage during the war. Its leaders, Vaughan and Parry, Brown and Richards, were drawn from different local churches. They became aware of the Council's plan for new, post-war housing estates. This work was most definitely a social reform and children's work, quite different from those created by revival people such as Powell of Plas Bennion, which became a private venture. Yet ultimately they affiliated with the Emmanuel Holiness Movement.

There was no westward penetration towards Ruthin or Denbigh and yet, a farm girl, from Gwyddelwern, knew of such a fellowship that was encouraged in the local Chapel. No details at all have been furnished about Gospel Halls or Mission Halls in North Clwyd or Flintshire. Members of the Emmanuel Bible College in the Wirral came over from about 1930 to conduct Evangelistic Crusades, but they were happy to use existing Methodist Halls. Their major message was, "Be separate, be sanctified and be holy!" What is more surprising is the great gap, along the Clwydian coast to Colwyn Bay. This record has had to creep over the boundary into Gwynedd in order to cover the witness at the Adelphi Hotel and also, the Mission, called the Iron Tabernacle.

Mr. Powell Parry, interviewed by the Rev. Cook a few years ago, said that the local people began to reject Mission Halls. They sent their children to places where they could get acquainted with new philosophies and theories. He said bitterly that, in weeknight meetings, people were happy enough to debate but not to testify or praise. His explanation can be compared with the situation in West Wales, only one generation after the Revival. There, once the old deacons and elders had gone, they demanded ministers with M.A's, B.A's and B.D's to tell them about social issues as taught to the ministers in the college. Eventually, modernism came in like an avalanche though these new ministers and teachers did not overstress things. After socialism came nationalism. The members wanted clever degreed men as their pastors and debates rather than meetings. They would not testify at experience meetings though they still said they were 'partaking of the means of grace.' The cumulative effect was a spiritual withering.

Welsh Language Mission Ventures in Gwynedd

A few of the Mission Halls already existed on the North coast under the direction of the Brethren, but the only one of which we have information, is Mr. Horace Jones' pioneer work at the Adelphi Mission in Llandudno. There was also a place on the eastern promenade, called the Iron Tabernacle, Queen Street. The next centre of any importance was Llanfairfechan, near to Bangor. Thanks to Peter and Dorothy Bennett, who recovered forgotten documents, we can see the embryonic form of an Independent Mission. John Owen reported a type of outreach Mission, which invited and catered for women. It went on meeting for years at Nant school and then moved to cottages when the older converts were, often, all too poorly to venture out. John Owen recalled very emotional meetings at Mrs. Bates' Scripture-saturated addresses at Felin Newydd and the occasional joyous service, which was attended by visitors. Gradually, the Rapture and the Return of Christ were becoming the chief themes. Three notable women showed increasing boldness and authority on this theme.

All through the Welsh-speaking province of Gwynedd, we have discovered only three Mission Halls. The one in the poorest part of Bangor was motivated by the visiting preacher, Rev. W.S. Jones. Speaking to the students, who had experienced personal revival, he challenged them to set up a compassionate and evangelistic work there, just as his wife was doing in the Rhondda, at the Lamb Mission. It must have lapsed since then, as it is not mentioned in any denominational journal. Many years later, a Pentecostal group held mini-crusades, which resulted in a small assembly.

In a period of growing scepticism, they believed that the only effective approach was personal challenge on the streets and markets anywhere. Eventually there was a little Assembly Room in East Bangor, similar to the one in English speaking Holyhead, which had a woman prophet during the war but did not come to evangelise the mainland until the fifties.

The two Halls that existed in Caernarfon, before the last War were very different. Down in Mark Lane, near the oldest cinema, a Mission was set up, whose express purpose was to reach and teach roughly clad and rough-tongued children. Those who chose to become disciples of Christ in their youth could be transferred to Pendref chapel, on the hill.

Already, in 1900, there was another building, called 'Feed My Lambs.' The original site was long since decayed and covered with ivy, but the work continued in a building near the National school, somewhere near the infants' department. In the late twenties, Stephen Jeffreys came there and conducted an evangelistic Mission. After using the Pavilion for healing meetings for the converts of this Mission, they seem to have rented the Church Hall premises and continued their work from there for about ten years.

That was the end of the road for Mission Halls in Welsh Wales, which would have seemed a strange beast to the average Welsh speaking Christian. The needs that the believers felt in South and East Wales were not felt in the land of great conservative chapels. Can we repeat, at the conclusion, that those needs included compassion, soul winning, defence of the Word and a perpetual search for new dimensions of spirit- filled life.

20 *Do we still need the Missions and Gospel Halls?*

One hundred years after these strange buildings appeared, many Christian leaders are suggesting that their day is over, that their support is melting away, that God has set them aside and that He is 'now doing a new thing.' Curiously enough, the same arguments were used long, long ago by established churches. Now, the new evangelicals use this kind of 'rejective' language, whether of the charismatic type, or the aggressive, judgmental, Puritan type. It would be far wiser to listen to the warnings quoted by one historian, "Beware of despising the day of little things."

One of our tragic errors, shared by one or more groups, is to take hold of Dr. Lloyd Jones's famous call to come out and be separate and to use it to ostracise several truly evangelical groups, who adore the same Lord and obey the same Spirit. The Doctor wanted us all to make a final public exit from traditional denominations, whose member churches had endorsed several forms of modernism and had thus forfeited their right to hold a candlestick, as John foresaw. Did Dr. Martin Lloyd Jones think we would break fellowship with born-again believers?

This separationist attitude suited many Gospel Halls and Mission Halls, who casually or deliberately ignored each other. The three main offshoots of the Brethren ran separate programmes, separate witness and separate conferences. In Llanelli, there were three unconnected Gospel Halls. In Cardiff, as early as 1919, there were five independent Gospel Halls, one of which now calls itself 'Evangelical Church.' Those, in Aberdare, meet in three types of Mission. Because of the usual ageing and 'population drift' tendencies that have bedevilled all bodies, each of the groups, in the old industrial districts, have shrunk to about a dozen each, with no young workers.

It is noticeable in Gwent that Methodists have rationalised the number of 'societies' and that the Pentecostals prefer to crowd into one or two centres, such as Crosskeys Tabernacle and the Cardiff City Temple. Perhaps this is something of which Christ would approve, this closer unity of His disciples.

Having visited about forty Mission Halls and Gospel Halls, one gets a better idea of the rate of decline and a reason why they have a predicted life of about ten years. Does this mean that their witness and teaching is not relevant, or is it caused by general lack of vision? A veteran complained bitterly, "Why are they dropping the title 'Gospel Hall' and using the name 'Evangelical Church' instead?" His explanation was that the present and coming generations were 'ashamed of the Gospel.'

We have reached the age of take-overs, when about twenty of the old independent missions, such as Penyrheol and Hengoed, Bush in Clydach and even Pisgah in Loughor are affiliated to A.E. C., F.I.E.C. and Free Ulster Presbyterian They have ceased to be truly independent.

What then do we owe to the Mission Halls and Gospel Halls? The question could be put to Mr. Selwyn Hughes of World-wide Revival, to Rev. David Shepherd, evangelist Bryn Jones, to J. Roderick Davies the pioneer Bible teacher in Southern Brazil, to Rev. Geraint Fielder and to Rev. Brynmor Jones.

Firstly they safeguarded their pulpits and platform and made sure that 'streams of pure living water' refreshed the souls of saints, even while they were absorbing in the Word of God. That effect was enhanced at their prayer meetings, if open to other believers.

About half of them gave proper thought to the status and role of the 'sisters.' Two kinds of Mission still say, "Let the women be silent," whereas another nearby Gospel Hall would have testimonies and prophecies and even recognised Gospel singers, similar to those in the 1904 Revival.

The power of the church or assembly meeting was reasserted as against pyramids of elders, deacons etc. or the unstable rule of house-fellowship leaders. They have long since proved the worth of their 'weekly fishing' with pamphlets, open-air meetings and the now popular 'March of Witness.'

The rapid growth of many independent Missions in unattractive areas showed that God could grow good fruit trees on barren land. A few of them could be called born leaders or skilled evangelists, yet they sowed and planted until they could do no more. Their children neglected this task of witness and there seemed to be no new leaders to inspire them when the Depression and the War removed one generation from Wales.

The true values of these numerous ventures were to emphasise again. "'Not by might but by my Spirit,' saith the Lord." No wonder that one of my keenest, best-informed searchers wrote, quite recently, "Unless today's evangelical Christians are visited by the same powerful Holy Spirit, I fear we will remain as cold and weak as we are at present."

Appendix A: Foundation Document for four originals

New Text Document (2)

APPENDIX 1. Foundation Documents for four roriginals.

1.The first fellowship at Penygroes:
Welsh Original.

Rheolau ac Amodau Llywodraethol.
a luniwyd o dan nawdd y Weithred Trosglwyddiadol dyddiedig Hydref 14eg 1909, gan yr Ymddiriedolwyr apwyntiedig dros yr Adeilad a elwir 'Mission Hall' neu 'Yr Eglwys Efangylaidd'.

1. Y mae y Weithred Trosgwyddiadol yn caniatau adeiladu Neuadd Genhadol, heb fod yn Enwadol, at wasanaeth pwrpasol, yn unol a'r Rheolau ac Amodau Llwydraethol y rhai a luniwyd gan yr Ymddiriedolwyr, neu Bwyllgor apwyntiedig gan y cyfryw.

2. Yn gymaint a bod y Neuadd Genhadol wedi ei hadeiladu i'r pwrpas arbennig, sef Pregethu yr Efengyl, ac hefyd i gael cymdeithas a chymundeb, BYDDED HYN YN HYSBUS ei bod yn anenwadol, heb fod yn perthyn i unrhyw Sect arbennig. Felly ni chaniata yr Ymddiriedolwyr i ynrhyw berson neu bersonau i wyro oddiwrth y Rheolau a'r Amodau Llywodraethol a lunwyd gan yr Ymddiriedolwyr.

3. Mae rhyddid perffaith i addoli mewn Ysbryd a Gwirionedd, yn unol a GAIR YSGRIFENEDIG DUW. Os bydd i unrhyw berson neu bersonau wrthryfela yn erbyn y Rheolau cydnabyddedig, rhaid fydd i'r Arweinwyr swyddogol a ddewisid gan y Cynhulliad ddelio a'r cyfryw. Os na lwyddir i gymodi, bydd yn ofynnol i alw i fewn yr Ymddiriedolwyr; dyfarniad y cyfrew fydd yn derfynol.

4. Parthed Cyfarfodydd Arbennig:- y mae pob rhyddid i'r aelodau i alw a rhoi cyhoeddiad i unrhyw un a fyddo brofedig fel Gwas Duw yn ol y Testament Newydd, pa un bynnag ai 'Pastor', neu 'Parchedig', 'Esgob' neu 'Offeiriad', neu unrhyw Frawd neu Frodyr, ar y telerau fod eu bywyd yn gyson a'u Proffes, ac yn dwyn tystiolaeth i ras achubol Duw.

5. Y mae o'r pwys mwyaf i ddal sylw fod perffaith ryddid i Wragedd neu Chwiorydd i weddio, tystiolaethu, a chanu emynau ysbrydol, ac addoli Duw mewn Ysbryd a Gwyrionedd, megys ag y cynhyrfer hwy gan yr Ysbryd Glan. Hefyd y mae perffaith ryddid i Genhades, neu chwaer a fyddo yn Efengyles, i gyhoeddi y Newyddio Da o lawenydd mawr, megys Mair, yr hon a gafodd gomisiwn i ddwyn tystiolaeth i'r Atgyfodiad: "Eithr dos at Fy mrodyr a

6. Bydd yn ofynnol i'r Aelodau i fod yn gyfrifol am bob treuliau i gadw yr Adeilad (I fewn ac allan) mewn cyflwr gweddus, ac i dalu yr holl ddyledion a ofynnir o bryd i bryd, yn ol dyfarniad y Rheolau a luniwyd gan yr Ymddiriedolwyr; y cyfryw daliadau (Ynghyd a'r 'Fire Insurance Premium') i'w cymeryd fel ac yn lle y tal dyledys o 'Rent' ar hyd y bydd y cynhulliad yn ddeiliaid yn y 'Mission Hall'.

Arwyddwyd ar rhan yr YMDDIRIEDOLWYR,
REES EVANS.
Cadeirydd, ac Ysgrifennydd.

Rules and regulations.
for the management and government of the Mission Hall, Penygroes (Non sectarian), commonly known as "Yr Eglwys Efengylaidd", as framed by the present Trustees under the provisions of the Trust Deed, dated 14th. Oct. 1909.

Note: The Trust Deed permitted the Erection of a Mission Hall to be used for non-sectarian purposes according and subject to such rules and regulations for the management and government of the same as shall be from time to time hereafter framed by the Trustees or by a Committee appointed or approved by them."

1. Any and every person or persons desiring to have fellowship or to worship at the above EGLWYS efengylaidd" must strictly conform to the Rules and Regulations hereby set forth by the Trustees.
2. Inasmuch as this Mission Hall was originally built for a specific purpose namely to preach the Gospel of our Lord and Saviour Jesus Christ and to evangelise and also to hold fellowship and Communuion and was therefore named 'The Evangelical Church', BE IT KNOWN that it is NON_SECTARIAN and UNDENOMINATIONAL. therefore on no account do the Trustees allow any person or persons to deviate from the terms of the Trust Deed and the Rules and Regulations laid down by the Trustees.
3. There shall be perfect liberty to worship in Spirit and in Truth in accordance with the Written Word of God. Any person or persons rebelling against this rule or interrupting the services must be dealt with by the Leaders or Officers chosen by the Assembly worshipping at the said Evangelistic church. Failing a satisfactory agreement, the Trustees should be called upon to give their final decision.
4. Regarding the holding of Special Services, there is

liberty to call and engage an accredited Servant of God who is a Minister of the New Testament, whether he be a Pastor, a minister of the Church of England, or any lay brother or person provided his life accords with his profession and that he has a vital testimony witnessing to the saving grace of God in salvation.

5. It is also most important to note and observe that there should be perfect liberty for the women and sisterhood(as urged and led by God, the Holy Spirit) to pray and to testify and sing spiritual songs unto the Lord and to worship God in Spirit and in Truth.

6. The people who assemble at the Evangelistic Church are to be responsible for all expenses of upkeep and maintenance of the Mission Hall and Outbuildings in decent condition, and also to be responsible for all expenses incurred as necessary in all matters, arising from time to time, in accordance with the Rules and Regulations from time to time framed by the Trustees under the powers of the said Trust Deed.

7. In order that the Trustees may attend to and pay for certain items of expense and cost in relation to the structure of the said Mission Hall and outbuildings, the Trustees impose a weekly rent of --------- to be paid every quarter on the usual quarter days (25th.March, 24th.June, 29th September, and 25th December) of each year commencing from the 1st.January,1958 and to be paid to Pastor Rees Evans, Gwalia Stores, Penygroes, (as Secretary to the Trustees) whose receipt shall be a sufficient discharge for such rent.

Ffurfwyd yr Eglwys Efengylaidd yn No 4. Dobell Terrace, yn nhy Henry Richards, ar y Drydedd Sul o Awst, 1907, ar ol dychwelyd o Cynhadledd Llandrindod, Yr oedd yn bresenol yn y Cwrdd cyntaf, Henry Richards a Susannah Richards, Ebenezer Griffiths a Eleanor Griffiths, William Roderick James, John David Daniels a Mary Ann Daniels, William Rees a Lizzie Ann Rees, David Evans a Ann Evans, David Davies, Pantybas, Daniel Thomas Glaspant a Mrs. Mary Oliver, Tycanol, Penygroes a Mrs. Catherin Roberts, Ty-uchaf, Penygroes a'i chwaer Mrs. Hollins. Yr hon oedd yn bydoesi a Geirge Muller, Bristol, yr hon a rhoddodd y Fan Efengylaidd i wasanaeth yr Efengyl trwy Gymru, ag fe etholwyd Mr. Willie Evans o Bontypridd i Efengylu arni. Pwysleisir gan y Frawdoliaeth, ailenedigaeth a Sicrwydd Cadwedigaeth a Sancteiddiad ac ail Ddyfodiad yr Arglwydd Iesu Grist ac yno y Biwyd hyd agorwyd y Neuadd Efengylu yn 1910.

Appendix B: Ynysafan

THE YNYSAFON GOSPEL MISSION.
CWMAVON.
RULES.

NAME THE YNYSAFON FREE GOSPEL MISSION.
FREE MEANS 'UNDENOMINATIONAL'
SERVICES. THE SERVICES SHALL BE IN WELSH AND ENGLISH.

DOCTRINES AND TEACHINGS.
(A). THAT NONE OTHER THAN THE TRINITY BE PREACHED IN THIS MISSION.
(B). THE FATHERHOOD OF GOD AND THE FELLOWSHIP OFTHE HOLY SPIRIT
(C). THE DIVINITY OF OUR SAVIOUR JESUS CHRIST.
(D). NO UNITARIAN TEACHING IS ALLOWED TO BE TAUGHT, PREACHED OR PRACTISED IN THIS MISSION HALL.
(E). THAT THERE IS NO TONGUE TO BE TAUGHT, PREACHED OR PRACTISED IN THIS CHURCH.

CHURCH OFFICERS.
(A). THE CHURCH MEMBERS WILL HAVE POWER TO APPOINT OFFICERS.
(B). NO OFFICERS WILL BE APPOINTED, ONLY BY ELECTION OF CHURCH MEMBERS.
(C). THAT THE OFFICERS SHALL OBSERVE CHURCH DISCIPLINE AND ORDER.
(D). SISTERS CAN BE ELECTED AS OFFICERS IN THE PROPORTION OF THREE TO FOUR OF THE NUMBER OF MEN APPOINTED OFFICERS.

PASTOR.
HE SHALL,AT ALL TIMES, BE SUBJECT TO THE RULING OF THE CHURCH. THE RULING OF THREE MONTHS NOTICE ON EITHER SIDE SHALL BE DEEMED NECESSARY.

CHURCH HALL.
THAT THE MISSION HALL IS NOT TO BE UTILISED FOR POLITICAL PURPOSES, OR FOR ANY AMUSEMENTS SUCH AS DANCING AND WHIST DRIVES.

VOTING. IN THE CASE OF VOTING, THREE-FOURTHS OF THE CHURCH MEMBERS SHALL BE OBSERVED AS THE RULING FIGURE.

GENERAL RULES.

(1). EVERY MEMBER IS EXPECTED TO ATTEND COMMUNION EVERY MONTH. IF THREE COMMUNIONS IN SUCCESSION ARE LOST, REASON FOR THIS COMMISSION MUST BE SUBMITTED TO THE DEACONS OF THE CHURCH.
(2). EVERY MEMBER IS EXPECTED TO ATTEND THE CHURCH SERVICES AS OFTEN AS POSSIBLE.

(3). EVERY MEMBER IS EXPECTED TO LIVE AN UNDEFILED LIFE AND TO FOLLOW THE MASTER'S EXAMPLE OF LIFE AS NEAR AS POSSIBLE.
(4). NO MEMBER IS ALLOWED TO BE A MEMBER OF A CLUB, OR BE A STEWARD OF SAME, OR BE A LANDLORD OF A PUBLIC HOUSE AND BE A MEMBER OF THIS CHURCH. NEITHER IS A MEMBER ALLOWED TO PARTICIPATE IN GAMBLING OF ANY KIND.
(5). NO MEMBER IS ALLOWED TO TRANSFER HIS OR HER MEMBERSHIP TO OTHER CHURCHES AND BE RE-INSTATED IN THIS CHURCH WITHOUT CONSIDERATION OF THEIR MEMBERSHIP BY THE DEACONS.
(6). IT WILL BE DEEMED PRUDENT FOR EVERY MEMBER OF THE CHURCH NOT TO DIVULGE ANY OF THE BUSINESS OF THE CHURCH.
(7). LETTERS WILL BE GIVEN AND RECEIVED CONCERNING MEMBERSHIP.
(8). BAPTISMAL RIGHTS. WE BELIEVE IN BAPTISM BY IMMERSION IN WATER AND THE BAPTISM OF SPRINKLING OF WATER TO CHILDREN.

SIGNED ON BEHALF OF THE YNYSAFON FREE GOSPEL MISSION.

LEWIS WILLIAMS, IVOR THOMAS, JAMES MARKS,
DAVID THOMAS, MOSES POWELL, EDWARD MORGAN,
DAVID CHARLES PRICE, JOSHUA SAMUEL,
WILLIAM REES, (PASTOR.)
DAVID J. PHILLIPS. (SECRETARY).

Appendix C: A Statement of Fundamental Truths

A STATEMENT OF

FUNDAMENTAL TRUTHS

APPROVED BY THE GENERAL COUNCIL OF ASSEMBLIES OF GOD IN GREAT BRITAIN AND IRELAND.

The Scriptures, known as the Bible, are the Inspired Word of God, the infallible and all-sufficient rule for faith, practice, and conduct. This Statement of Fundamental Truths is not intended as a creed for the Church, but as a basis of unity for a full Gospel Ministry (1 Cor. 1, 10).

1. The Bible is the Inspired Word of God. (2 Tim. 3, 15-16: 2 Peter 1, 21).
2. The Unity of The One True and Living God Who is the Eternal, Self-Existent "I AM," Who has also revealed Himself as One Being in three Persons, Father, Son and Holy Spirit. (Deut. 6, 4; Mark 12, 29; Matt. 28, 19).
3. The fall of man, who was created pure and upright, but fell by voluntary transgression. (Gen. 1, 26-31; 3, 1-7; Rom. 5, 12-21).
4. Salvation through faith in Christ, Who died for our sins according to the Scriptures, was buried, and was raised from among the dead on the third day according to the Scriptures, and through His Blood we have Redemption. (Tit. 2, 11; 3, 5-7; Rom. 10, 8-15; 1 Cor. 15, 3-4). This experience is also known as the New Birth, and is an instantaneous and complete operation of the Holy Spirit upon initial faith in the Lord Jesus Christ. (John 3, 5-6; James 1, 18; 1 Peter 1, 23; 1 John 5, 1.)
5. Baptism by immersion in water is enjoined upon all who have really repented and have truly believed with all their hearts in Christ as Saviour and Lord. (Matt. 28, 19; Acts 10, 47-48; Acts 2, 38-39.)
6. The Baptism in the Holy Spirit, the initial evidence of which is the speaking with other tongues as the Spirit gives utterance. (Acts 2, 4; 10, 44-46; 11, 14-16; 19, 6; Isa. 8, 18).
7. Holiness of life and conduct in obedience to the command of God, "Be ye holy for I am holy." (1 Peter 1, 14-16; Heb. 12, 14; 1 Thess. 5, 23; 1 John 2, 6; also 1 Cor. 13).
8. Deliverance from sickness, by Divine Healing, is provided for in the Atonement. (Isa. 53, 4-5; Matt. 8, 16-17.)
9. Breaking of Bread is enjoined upon all believers until the Lord comes. (Luke 22, 14-20; 1 Cor. 11, 20-34).
10. The pre-millennial second coming of the Lord Jesus Christ is the blessed hope set before all believers. (1 Cor. 15, 22-24; 1 Thess. 4, 13-18; 1 Cor. 15, 51-57).
11. Everlasting punishment is the portion of all who are not written in the Book of Life. (Rev. 20, 10-15).
12. The Gifts of the Holy Spirit and the Offices have been set by God in the Church as recorded in the New Testament. (1 Cor. 12, 4-11, 28; Eph. 4, 7-16).

Appendix D: List of Informants

Chapter	Area	Informant
1	West Wales	Mr Perkins
2	Penygroes	The late Meurig Thomas
3	East Dyfed	The late Meurig Thomas
		Mr Ron Perkins
		Mrs Davies (Cwmgwili)
		Mrs Doris Goronwy
4	Llanelli	Mrs Davies
		The late Mr Board
		Mr & Mrs Lewis Evans
5	Loughor Valley	Rev David Shepherd
		Mr Ron Perkins
		Mr Martyn Jones
		Mr & Mrs John Lewis
		Mrs Thomas
		Capt Lambert Jenkins
6	Tawe Valley	Pastor Len Sparkes
		David Meadows
		Clarence James Meadows
7	Swansea	Mrs Joseph
		Mr Wilf Beale
		Rev Rowlands
		The late Mr Roberts
8	Neath	Len Sparkes
		Mr & Mrs Rosser
9	Kenfig Ridge	Mr Ollerton
		Mr Loosemore
		Miss Loosemore
10	Bridgend	Mr Oswald Penry
		Mr Gerald Gray
		Mrs McHale
		Rev David Evans
		Mr and Mrs Locke

Chapter	Area	Informant
11	Rhondda	Mrs Beti Symons
		Mrs Rex
12	Cynon Valley	Mr. George Davies
		Mrs Eira Richards
		Mr Windsor Jones
		Mrs.Mabel Lewis
		Mr & Mrs Mitchell
		Mrs Jarvis
13	Taff Rhymney	Mr. Jack Webb
14	Western Gwent	Mrs Catherine Brown
		Pastor Palmer
		Mrs Megan Parry
15	East Gwent	Mrs Mills
		Cwmfelinfach
		Rev. Haydn Williams
		Mrs Audrey Jones
16	South Wales	Late Mrs W.S.Jones
		Late Thomas Wintle
		Rev Byron Llywellyn
17	Cardiff, Barry and Newport	Rev Brian Close
		Mr Hunt
		Mr Elliott
		Pastor Thomas
		Rev Dennis Monger
		Mr & Mrs David Woolley
18	Powys	Charles & Beryl Evans
		Mr Peter Beechey
19	Clwyd	Mrs Brown
20	Gwynedd	Mr Coe

SOURCE BOOKS

Griffiths. What God has wrought
Williams. William Herbert of Ammanford
Ollerton. Revivals children
Perkins. The Revival in East Carmarthenshire
Jones. Seventy Years at Cwmdare
Snelling. Swansea Mission
Webber. Lon Las Mission
Wintle. Five booklets
Echoes of Grace – Apostolic
Echoes of Service – Brethren

Other books by Brynmor Pierce Jones

The Kings Champions, Christian Literature Press, 1986
Sowing beside all waters, Cwmbran Community Press, 1985
The Spiritual History of Keswick in Wales 1903-1983, Christian Literature Press, 1989
An Instrument of Revival, Bridge Publishing, 1995
Voices of the Revival, Evangelical Press of Wales, 1995
The Trials and Triumphs of Mrs Jesse Penn Lewis, Bridge-Logos, 1997

Please note that further copies of this book can be ordered from:

Wellspring
39, Pillmawr Circle
Malpas
Newport
NP20 6WP

Tel: (01633) 856855
(01633) 422689